Praise for **THE 10-SECOND RULE**

"I've known Clare De Graaf for more than twenty years now. He is a great example of the transition from success (CEO of an industry-leading company) to significance (twenty-five years of mentoring men). *The 10-Second Rule* is a simple yet profound practice that could change your whole point of view on life. It works."

—Bob Buford, cofounder, Leadership Network,
and author of *Halftime*, *Finishing Well*, and
My Never Ending Blog (ActiveEnergy.net)

"Ephesians 2:10 tells us, 'For we are God's workmanship, created in Christ Jesus to do the work that He has prepared in advance for us to do.' In his book *The 10-Second Rule*, Clare encourages us to become so familiar with the voice of the Spirit of God, so in tune with His call, that we hasten to listen and obey. This has been Clare's lifestyle for many years as he mentors other men and sees many of them grow in Christ."

—Betty Huizenga, founder,
Apples of Gold Ministries

"I've known Clare for over twenty years. He's a passionate and devoted Jesus follower. This book is simple yet profound, and anyone who is interested in obeying Jesus will benefit."

—Edward Dobson, pastor emeritus,
~ry Church, Grand Rapids, MI

T0019276

"This author has been my guide and counsel for more than forty years, so I can testify that most of what he says about himself is true, with the following exceptions: He claims to be just a normal guy, when in fact he is probably the most extraordinary person I know. Furthermore, he confesses the sin of pride, but in fact I know him to be obedient to the Holy Spirit even when that obedience might humiliate him. This book is tangible evidence that the man who wrote *The 10-Second Rule* practices it himself, for it is only by Clare's obedience and God's provision that you are holding this book in your hand. May every reader be as blessed by this book as I have been by the God who conceived it and the man who penned it." (Dad, of course I didn't expect this to be published—I wrote it because I felt an impression to do so. I'm more proud of you than you'll ever know.)

—Jennifer Tendero, cofounder, Stockbridge Boiler Room Ministry

"Clare writes with a fresh honesty that is challenging us to think anew about what God wants us to do when confronted with certain opportunities and temptations. Read the book through. We expect you, too, will find yourself yearning to participate in an adventure you might otherwise never have dreamed about."

—John and Sarita Holzmann, cofounders, Sonlight Curriculum

"I have known Clare for over forty years and have been an accountability partner of his for the last fifteen. Clare's heart for God and for people is undeniable. The life he lives and perspective he shares has challenged and changed me. This book will challenge and change the way you engage with the world, I promise!"

—Dick DeVos, former president, Amway, and author of the bestselling book *Rediscovering American Values*

"This book can be life changing for those with the courage to take a step of faith. After reading *The 10-Second Rule* on vacation, Rita and I arrived at the airport for our flight home, and there was a woman with four little ones, trying to juggle a baby and get snacks for the other three. The nudge in my heart was to offer her a hand. To my surprise, she immediately accepted, sending me off to her table with pretzels and crackers, and thanked me warmly. An hour later, in the terminal, she spotted Rita and me near our gate and gave me the biggest and warmest thank you again for helping her. Such a simple step. . . . May the Lord get the glory."

—Roy Peterson, president and CEO, The Seed Company,
and former president, Wycliffe Bible Translators

THE 10 SECOND RULE

SECOND RULE

FOLLOWING JESUS MADE SIMPLE

CLARE DE GRAAF

HOWARD BOOKS
AN IMPRINT OF SIMON & SCHUSTER, INC.

New York • Nashville • London • Toronto • Sydney • New Delhi

Howard Books
An Imprint of Simon & Schuster, Inc.
1230 Avenue of the Americas
New York, NY 10020

First Howard Books trade paperback edition April 2015

HOWARD and colophon are trademarks of Simon & Schuster, Inc.

For information about special discounts for bulk purchases, please contact Simon & Schuster Special Sales at 1-866-506-1949 or business@simonandschuster.com.

The Simon & Schuster Speakers Bureau can bring authors to your live event. For more information or to book an event contact the Simon & Schuster Speakers Bureau at 1-866-248-3049 or visit our website at www.simonspeakers.com.

Designed by William Ruoto

Manufactured in the United States of America

10 9 8 7 6 5 4 3

Library of Congress Cataloging-in-Publication Data

De Graaf, Clare.
The 10-second rule™ : following Jesus made simple / Clare De Graaf.
    p. cm.
1. Obedience—Religious aspects—Christianity. I. Title. II. Title: Ten-second rule.
BV4647.O2D44 2013
248.4—dc23   2012031819

ISBN 978-1-4767-1508-7 (pbk)
ISBN 978-1-4767-0278-0 (ebook)

To my wife, Susan,
You have been a Proverbs 31 woman,
helping and advising me at every stage in this work.
I love you, my wife of forty-seven years. You are
the wind beneath my wings.

And to our children,
Jennifer, Molly, Megan, Betsy, Tyler, Veti,
and all their children,
thank you for making my quiver full,
and for being one of the great joys of my life.
I love you effortlessly.

CONTENTS

My Story—and Perhaps Yours As Well   xi

Part I: The Principles

CHAPTER ONE
A Rule of Life   3

CHAPTER TWO
Dueling Voices   17

CHAPTER THREE
Listening to the Voice of God   33

CHAPTER FOUR
Why Your Simple Obedience Matters   55

Part II: The Practices

CHAPTER FIVE
The Power of Small Beginnings   73

Contents

CHAPTER SIX
Pre-decisions   87

CHAPTER SEVEN
Love the One You're With   109

CHAPTER EIGHT
From a Rule of Life to a Lifestyle   123

Part III: The Preparation

CHAPTER NINE
The School of Jesus   145

CHAPTER TEN
Doing the Rule: 10₄30   161

CHAPTER ELEVEN
Why Bother?   179

And Without You . . .   191
Study Guide   195

My Story—and Perhaps Yours As Well

Up until age thirty-one, I was your standard-issue Christian—the kind the Christian schools and churches in our conservative town pounded out year after year like spiritual Model Ts—mostly in one color: beige. We were covenant children. So we figured we came with a cradle-to-grave salvational warranty.

And in the midsixties, high school seniors in my church were expected to make a public profession of their faith unless they were atheists or Democrats. I was neither. But I had questions.

So my parents called our pastor. A good man, really—kind, intelligent, but a man who could be deadly serious when he needed to be. "Our son's just not sure, Pastor. Maybe if you talked to him." So over he came to our house to work on me like I was the last holdout on a hung jury. My parents knew they needed a closer. And local legend had it that Reverend Jacob's win record stretched clear back to the Truman administration.

My parents sat in the room with us, praying, while Pastor Jake went to work. "Tell me, son—what's the problem?"

Well, the problem was that I didn't *feel* any real excitement for Jesus. I believed that everything in the Bible was true. I believed that Jesus was the Son of God, that he'd died on the cross, risen from the dead, and was coming back to judge the living and the dead. I bought the whole party line but felt no passion for God, no passion to live a life radically different from any other guy my age.

It just seemed to me that if I was going to make a public profession of my faith, the equivalent of adult baptism or confirmation in most churches, that I ought to have a little fire in my belly for God. I didn't. All I really cared about were girls and making a ton of money as fast as I could. Of course, I couldn't say *that* to the pastor, especially not in front of my parents, so I just stuck with the "I don't feel anything special" line.

I don't remember everything he said that day, but here's the gist of it: "Clare, if you believe that everything you've been taught about God is true, you have faith. You *are* a believer, even if you don't feel it right now."

I looked to my parents for support, but they were avoiding direct eye contact. They sensed that Jake was on the verge of victory, and they weren't about to break the cobra's stare.

I loved my parents more than God back then, so I caved. They were happy.

The pastor was happy.

I wasn't.

I felt like I was about to stand in front of the king and pledge my allegiance, even though I wasn't really in love yet with either him or his kingdom. It felt phony.

But Jake was the pastor, seminary trained and all, so who was I, a seventeen-year-old kid, to tell him what faith was?

So that June I became an official Christian.

It was one of the worst mistakes of my life.

In my mind I had my get-out-of-hell-free card. I just needed to keep loving God (whatever that meant), love others, attend church regularly, serve, give, keep a lid on the public sin in my life, and pray. I'd grown up in the church; I knew what was expected, and I did it. One more beige Christian parked in the pews waiting for my weekly fill-up.

You see, my people are Dutch. Responsible. Wary of spontaneity. We knew where that led. We'd seen them on Christian TV, with helmets of white hair, jumping up praising the Lord and making some pretty eyebrow-raising claims or predictions after getting a "word" from him. We were not about to let that happen to us—get ourselves bushwhacked by emotion or impetuous decisions. Ours was a sensible faith.

I don't blame my church, or my parents, or the Christian schools—they taught me truth and loved me well. I didn't even know I had a problem to blame anyone for. I just thought that's all there was to it—that's what it meant to be a Christian. God was close enough to be a comfort, but distant enough to not be terribly inconvenient.

"Clare, I'm sorry, but you have lymphoma cancer—five to nine years to live is my best guess." That emotional baseball bat swung by a doctor on an otherwise sunny day in August more than thirty years ago triggered a crisis of faith that finally forced me to take a second look at my life and at Jesus as I tried to figure out what I'd missed. And as I began rereading the Gospels, here's what started to trip me up:

"Do good to those who hate you."
"Deny yourself daily."
"I came not to be served, but to serve."
"But I say forgive seventy times seven."
"Whoever wants to be first . . . must become last."
"No man can serve two masters."
"Give to the one who asks you."
"Give no thought for tomorrow."

This Jesus who said these things appeared to be anything but sensible! Here was God himself in Jesus Christ inviting all who would enter his kingdom to abandon comfortable Christianity, to abandon the common sense I prized so highly, the very thing that governed my life. *Leave it at the door,* he was saying. *I'll meet you at the foot of the cross, where your old life will end and the new life I'll give you will begin. I'll issue you new instructions from there. Trust me—and come follow me.*

I found nothing in the Gospels that sounded even remotely like the church-on-Sundays-and-Wednesdays, believe-in-the-Bible, serve-on-some-committees plan.

The beige plan.

My plan.

What the Jesus of the Gospels seemed to be calling me to frightened and confused me, partly because it threatened the very survival of every aspect of my carefully planned life. Besides, I knew very few Christians who actually lived like that. I had always admired the few I did know in my church—the really gung-ho types. You know, the people always more than willing to serve anyone anytime, the first to sign up for a month-long missions trip to Mexico in the sweltering heat of summer. I cheered them on from the sidelines. I just didn't see the point, for myself, of being overly obedient or spiritual. I didn't need box seats in heaven—after all, how bad could the bleachers be? I was *in*.

Was I? The more I read the Bible, the only plan Jesus ever seemed to offer was: *I am the way, the truth, and the life. Deny yourself. Take up your cross daily and follow me. Imitate me. Love others more than yourself.* Apparently, the *gold* plan.

I spent months reading Scripture, counting the cost, sniffing around the trap, desperately trying to find Plan B—a less costly and less intrusive way to follow Jesus. But all the while, against my ever-weakening self-will, I felt drawn by the love of Jesus to go for it—both feet—all in!

I was thirty-one, the proverbial rich young ruler: husband, father of three, Sunday school teacher, deacon, a twice-on-Sunday Christian—when a bonfire of true faith was finally lit in me. To this day, I'm not sure if God simply fanned into flames the pilot light of faith I received as a child or if I was truly born again.

This much is certain: I fell in love with Jesus and repented of both my stubborn, sinful heart and much of my cultural Christianity. This time I gladly and unashamedly pledged my eternal allegiance to him and to his kingdom agenda.

God so transformed my life, my passions, and priorities that at age thirty-five, I sold my manufacturing business to devote the balance of my life to doing whatever it was God wanted of me. I've had steady work ever since.

For nearly three decades now, I've been a full-time volunteer spiritual mentor, meeting young men at Starbucks who have no interest in God, pointing wayward men back to their families, teaching the whole counsel of God, and all the while trying to keep God's reputation and mine intact.

It's great work, if you can get it. I love it.

Frankly, I Really Didn't Want to Write This Book

For years, people had been urging me to write a book about my life experiences, or the things I've taught. My stock response had always been: "The world really doesn't need one more Christian book."

Then one Sunday morning in 2010, after I'd finished my regular early morning time with God, I came back into our bedroom where my wife, Susan, was just waking up. Sitting on the edge of the bed I said softly, "You're not going to believe this."

She looked at me expectantly.

"I just got a strong impression as I was praying. I believe it was from God. I think he wants me to write a book."

She was incredulous. "But I thought you said you would never . . ."

"Yeah. I know. But think about it. Do I really have a choice? How would I explain to God someday why I refused to write a book on obedience? How's *that* for irony!"

"Do you have a title in mind?"

"I do. *The 10-Second Rule.*"

I'd been teaching the 10-Second Rule™ for a decade by then. I had learned about the Rule from Bill Job, a pastor working as a businessman in China. However, only weeks before that Sunday morning, one new follower of the 10-Second Rule suggested that I write a brief summary of the Rule to help him teach others. That's what I had been doing that very morning, until God showed up. Apparently he wanted more than a summary.

So, I left our bedroom and went back to writing. That's how this book began. Reluctantly.

Is this book for you?

Have you ever sat in church, wondering whether the person next to you is as bored with their Christian life as you are with yours? Of course you don't ask them, because good Christians shouldn't even think like that. You'd never walk away from it—after all, you love God. You believe the gospel. You enjoy the people at church.

You belong.

You hear inspiring stories of super-Christians leading people to Christ, or going off to Africa drilling for clean water, or doing other great things for God. You're happy for them, but by comparison you feel spiritually lifeless.

You've prayed for the Holy Spirit to rekindle the fire. You've been in and out of Bible studies, you volunteer in ministry, you've stopped and started reading through the Bible a half-dozen times. You've asked yourself if it could be your lukewarm friends, your daydreams of another life altogether, some secret sin, or some deep wound from the past—the one no one but God knows about—that's holding you back. You're frustrated because you truly want a more vibrant faith, but you don't have a clue how to get there from here.

I've written this book for people just like me.

My goal was to write a simple book, one that could be read in just a few hours, laying out exactly what it means to follow Jesus in real life. I hope I've done that. The theme of the book, obeying Jesus, isn't really all that complicated. Jesus' commands to us are pretty straightforward most of the time. It's the long list of excuses we effortlessly and creatively come up with to avoid obeying him that's at the heart of the problem.

In this book, I'll only rarely tell you what you must do other than inhale God's Word, which will point you toward the only formula that has ever worked—believing completely in the divinity and trustworthiness of Jesus and then making that the supreme purpose of your life to behave like him. That ought to be the normal Christian life. If that's not the ultimate purpose for our lives, we might as well go out and hit a bucket of golf balls on Sunday mornings.

If you're looking for a beautifully written book, or one that is deeply theological, this isn't it. But if you're interested in the hard-won lessons God has taught others and me and in the honest observations of an imperfect man who desperately longs to be more like Jesus, you may have found a friend.

So, that's how it is you find yourself reading this book. My prayer is that it inspires you to live with near reckless abandon this amazing adventure of following Jesus.

—*Clare De Graaf*

"Papa, what does it actually mean to be a follower of Jesus?"

"What do you think, Anders?"

"Well, I think it means to do everything Jesus tells us, even if we don't want to."

—Our grandson Anders, then age 10. Smart kid

PART I

The Principles

CHAPTER ONE

A Rule of Life

The Christian ideal has not been tried and found wanting.
It has been found difficult and left untried.

—G. K. CHESTERTON

The knock on the passenger-side window was so loud and unexpected it startled them both—father and son. That the father had been in the middle of an ATM withdrawal, cash in hand, only heightened his anxiety. But when he turned toward the sound of the knocking, his reflexes now on full alert, heart pounding, there was only a frail old woman standing at the passenger window, her nose nearly touching it, looking timid and more frightened than he was. The father almost laughed out loud. She'd scared the wits out of both of them! "Son, roll down your window, please," he said. For his son's sake he tried to sound more confident than he felt.

"Is there any way you could help me get some food for my grandchildren?" the old woman asked.

The father, a former lawyer recently turned pastor, was skeptical. He saw no reason to be afraid of this woman, but neither did he see any reason to trust that she was telling the truth. Was this a scam? It didn't help that his son, his face turned away from the woman only two feet behind him, pled desperately with his eyes: *No!*

The father recalled a conversation he and I had had only weeks before about why we're often so reluctant to simply obey God when he offers us unexpected or inconvenient assignments. This one seemed to qualify on both counts.

Nevertheless, he invited her to get in the car and they went off to the grocery store. As they were loading the bags in the trunk, the father made the mistake of asking if there was anything else she needed. Reluctantly, the woman mentioned that she also had a prescription for medication she couldn't afford. So of course more of the ATM cash disappeared at the pharmacy.

When the father offered to drive her and her groceries home, she was both surprised and grateful. She sat quietly in the backseat for most of the trip, but as they neared her home, she asked, "You're Christians, aren't you?"

"We are," he said.

"I thought so. Just before I saw your car at the ATM, I was sitting on the bench at the bus stop and I asked Jesus to send me a Christian."

As father and son pulled away from the old woman's house, the son asked a million questions, and the father realized that more had gone on than simply meeting another person's needs. His obedience had created a teachable moment. The son wasn't convinced that this had been the *smartest* thing his dad had ever done, but he was at least impressed with his father's spontaneous generosity and willingness to obey God.

Almost all of us have done similar things from time to time: random acts of grace and generosity. They make us feel alive, don't they? That's because they give us a taste, a glimpse, of what we were really created for.

It's like one of those ads on TV for a new car that

they've not yet released. They're teasing us, tempting us with flashing images as the new model passes through stands of trees, reflected in mirror-smooth lakes. The maker wants to whet our appetites.

Your maker does, too. And if you ignore your comfort zone long enough to jump at the chance to be spontaneously generous and kind when God throws those opportunities your way, you may be prompted to ask, *What if I could actually live like this every day? Not just giving away money, but giving myself away? What if these spontaneous acts of kindness and obedience happened so frequently, maybe a dozen times a week, that they become as natural and habitual as brushing my teeth or checking my email?*

The answer is that you'd be experiencing the natural consequence of a surrendered life. And in the divine math of the kingdom, when we give ourselves away, we actually discover our true purpose for life—the *normal Christian life.*

If you do, your legacy will be a string of a thousand stories, just like these:

A woman stood in the checkout line at the supermarket. The poor woman right in front of her, the one trying to corral three small children, was having a melt-down. It was every young mother's nightmare and then some.

One of her children was standing, runny nose and all, in the now-empty shopping cart; another was wailing at around a hundred decibels and hugging mom's leg like it was a tree in a hurricane; a third had run off somewhere. Meanwhile, the frantic young mom's only credit card had been denied. She'd dumped half the contents of her purse onto the grocery belt and was desperately pawing through the clutter of keys, crumpled receipts, makeup, and baby gear, trying to find enough cash to pay for the groceries, now bagged and ready. Like any good mother, she was also scanning the area for her missing son, in full panic mode.

The unfortunate mom appeared to be in her early thirties, but time and life had not been gentle. The lines on her face, the limp strands of hair now strag-gling across it, and the cheap clothes she wore screamed *poor*—poor financially and poor in spirit. If to such be-longs the kingdom of heaven, in the next life she might be queen. But right now, hope for anything other than day-to-day survival had fled; hers was the face of desperation. Suddenly she slowed and stopped, both hands in the pile of purse contents on the checkout counter, eyes staring blankly downward at nothing, as if she had reached the end of her energy and of whatever momentum had been carrying her forward.

The woman behind her who'd been watching quietly spoke. "Here, this ought to take care of it." She handed the clerk her credit card. The clerk looked from the credit card to the startled young mother. Neither seemed to know what to do next.

"You don't have to do that," the mother said, swiping the hair out of her face. She looked even more embarrassed than before. Finding her drive once again, she resumed clawing through the pile from her purse.

"No, I'm serious," said the woman in line, discreetly enough to preserve what little was left of the mother's dignity. "Please let me do this for you—and for your children." She motioned for the clerk to complete the transaction. "I'll watch your groceries if you want to go find your son."

The young mother was clearly struggling to understand what had just happened, but with that reminder, her mothering instincts kicked in. After a quick, embarrassed "Thanks," she hurriedly dumped her stuff back into her purse and, with one child in her arms and the other clasped tightly by the hand, rushed off in search of her lost lamb.

A few moments later, when the Good Samaritan saw the mother returning, family restored, she turned to leave.

"Stop, please," called the young mother. Dragging her three still-squabbling children up to the cart of bagged groceries, she said to the woman standing next to them, "Thank you so much, but have we met?"

The woman smiled. "No, I don't recall seeing you before."

"But then why did you offer to pay for my groceries?"

"I'm a Christian," the woman said simply. "As I stood behind you, I sensed that God was telling me to pay for your groceries, so I did. Simple as that. Since everything I have belongs to God anyway, *he* paid your bill—not me. Just thank him, if you'd like. I hope you have a great day." And with one last smile, the woman turned and left.

In the same way, let your light shine before men, that they may see your good deeds and glorify your Father in heaven. (Matthew 5:16)

Simple Obedience Isn't Always

In the two stories I've shared, God gave directions to his children—and they listened and obeyed. Simple as that. But it's not really that simple, is it?

At least, it never has been for me.

Even though I've been serious about following Jesus for more than thirty years now, there have been times when I've been just plain worn-out from life, difficult relationships, even from ministry, from being handed one more "opportunity to serve" because "you're so good at it." And worn-out from trying desperately, at the same time, to stomp out these little brushfires of sin that I knew were holding me back, denying me the joy of my salvation. So, periodically, I would give myself a breather and take a break from serious obedience. I just wanted to veg!

Using some internal moral-actuarial table, I would credit myself for church attendance, having personal devotions, giving, and generally being a good guy—with offsetting debits for sin. In my mind, and my arrogance, I assumed I had a positive balance compared to most other Christians I knew. I figured I had plenty of carry-forwards.

So I'd spend a few months waiting around for the Holy Spirit to do what I couldn't (and maybe didn't even really want to, at that time), ignite the fire once again. And that was fine with me. That way I could lay the responsibility for my lukewarm spirituality at *his* feet; it's up to God to jump-start my spiritual life. I wanted a Road to Damascus experience. Until I got it, I was content to sit out a few innings—just happy to be on the team.

Those grand epiphanies rarely came. What frightened me more than anything was being spiritually flat for so long that after a while I'd get used to it. It scared me to think that I might end up like so many I'd known, whose central purposes in life appeared to be killing time pleasantly in warm places, doing a little volunteer work, oh, and of course going to church.

Nobody wakes up one morning and makes the decision to be a lukewarm, religious Christian. So, I have a theory. I think we Christians who were once on fire for God often slowly and unconsciously drift toward religious activities, even good ones, because they're relatively convenient and culturally acceptable forms of obedience. It's a faith we can schedule into our busy lives—worship at 10:00 a.m., drop our offerings in the plate, Bible study on Tuesdays, volunteer on Wednesdays at 7:00 p.m. It's a spirituality that we can measure ourselves and others by—familiar and predictable, and it still leaves 95 percent of our waking hours for ourselves. Just the ticket for a user-friendly religion.

Eventually I would come to my senses and spend a few days alone doing serious business with God, crying out to him to forgive my spiritual laziness. And he would, of course. But it troubled me that he had to. Was this a cycle to which I had to simply resign myself?

A Rule of Life

Then a dozen years ago I was introduced to a rule of life so stunningly simple it was almost embarrassing. It gave me a place to begin again when I found myself spiritually on the bench. Its power is in its simplicity, and yet it gets straight to the heart of what it means to actually follow Jesus. It has become the rule for my life, just as it had for the followers of Jesus you met in the preceding stories.

A *rule of life* is just what it sounds like: a motto, vow, or promise which, if lived out courageously and consistently, at some point changes us from who we are to the men and women we truly long to become. *Rules of life* have been around as long as there have been people who longed to live lives pleasing to God. Samson, St. Francis of Assisi, the Moravians, Billy Graham, and others have all adopted them—simple statements of how they believe God intends them to live. Those rules become a compass, helping guide those who follow them to true spiritual north.

The 10-Second Rule is a rule of life. In living by it, you'll either become a far more serious follower of Jesus or realize fairly quickly that you just don't have much interest.

Obviously, I have no idea where you are on your

faith journey. You may still be kicking tires spiritually, still checking Jesus out. Or maybe you're disappointed with God right now because he hasn't yet delivered you from the wreckage you or others have made of your life. Perhaps you've been a Christian all your life but have resigned yourself to "this is as good as it's going to get." Please don't!

What is it that causes one believer in Jesus to become a passionate follower, someone whose life significantly impacts other lives, and another to settle for a life of beige Christianity?

A decision.

A personal decision to be far more serious about being like Jesus, whether anyone else in your life is or not.

Jesus' call to *come follow me* hasn't changed in two thousand years. The Rule isn't a new command. It's simply an easy-to-understand, to-the-point reminder of what it actually means to be on this journey with Jesus, to be led by him day by day, minute by minute—or even in the next ten seconds!

The **10** Second Rule™

Just do the next thing you're reasonably certain Jesus wants you to do.

[and commit to it immediately—in the next 10 seconds—
before you change your mind!]

"If you love me, you will obey what I command."

—JOHN 14:15

The Lay of the Land

I've divided this book into three parts, or sections. In the balance of this section of the book, which I've entitled "The Principles," and over the next few chapters, I'll introduce you to the five foundational principles that make the 10-Second Rule work in real life. Then, in "The Practices" section, you'll find all kinds of stories that give flesh to the Rule in ways that may surprise you. Finally, in "The Preparations," I'll share helpful ideas that will encourage you to prepare yourself to live with renewed hope and anticipation on this amazing journey following Jesus!

CHAPTER TWO

Dueling Voices

Everybody eventually surrenders to something or someone.
If not to God, you will surrender to the opinions or expectations
of others, to money, to resentment, to fear, or to your own pride,
lusts, or ego.

—*RICK WARREN, IN* THE PURPOSE-DRIVEN LIFE

Years ago, I began to notice that I would often feel an impulse to do something good that was out of the ordinary and out of my comfort zone. Maybe it was an impulse to stop to help a motorist broken down on the road, or visit a person in the hospital with few friends, or give money to a family whose tragic story I'd read in the newspaper, or talk to a co-worker about Jesus, or send an encouraging note to someone who appeared to need it badly.

Often it was something even more personal:

A friend asks me to pray for her. I say I will, of course, and even feel an inner urging to do it right then so I won't forget. But I don't. (Nor do I remember to do it later.)

I spot a new person in church, standing all alone. I have a strong impression—from God?—that I should leave my friends and welcome them.

I'm sitting at my computer and a pop-up tempts me to go to a website no Christian man ever should, and I immediately have an impulse to delete the message.

You get it. We've all had these impulses. Sometimes I would act on them, but far too often I wouldn't.

Why?

I know why. Because just about the time I heard that first voice, that inner urging, I heard another:

Clare, you can't save every person who has a need. Besides, you'll be late for your meeting. They probably have a cell phone—they can call a friend to help.

Be careful—that person is very emotionally needy.

Helping him could get messy. He'll want to be your best friend.

Don't say anything—you'll just embarrass them.

I'm sure that need will be met by someone else.

It's likely that family has insurance. And if not, good friends or some government agency will help them.

Who are you to judge whether that person is a believer?

Just one more time won't kill you.

You know that voice. My guess is you've heard it yourself.

It's the voice of reason, I assured myself. It helps rescue me from foolish impulses. Its job is to make sure I don't do anything stupid or embarrassing to myself or others, and that I don't get taken advantage of or miss out on some private pleasure I feel I'm entitled to. It's the safe voice—the smart voice—the guardian of sensible obedience.

It's likely the same voice the priest and the Levite heard on their way to Jericho.

And I've noticed something else: if this little debate going on in my heart and mind lasts long enough, the impulse to obey the first voice fades away. The broken-down car disappears in my rearview mirror. I arrive at my meeting and move on to other things. The paper goes out with the trash. A prayer request is forgotten.

And that initial impulse to do something good for another human being passes. Life moves on—comfortable and predictable.

It's disobedience by default; I simply have to do nothing.

This other voice has a thousand ready-made excuses, all more logical, convenient, or pleasurable, from which I effortlessly choose—and usually did.

So, the first, almost embarrassingly simple but foundational principle that makes following Jesus using the 10-Second Rule work in real life is this: *When you're reasonably certain Jesus is asking you to do something—do it immediately!* (Hence the 10 seconds.) Waiting just gives you a chance to overthink these impressions from God, giving doubt and fear an immediate opportunity to ask their questions and whisper their advice.

And when that happens, the other voice usually wins!

Just Who Is This Other Voice?

In the seventies, Flip Wilson, a well-known comedian, had a popular weekly TV show. One regular feature was a skit in which Flip was the fiery preacher Reverend LeRoy, constantly warning his congregation about the devil's plans to lead 'em all straight to hell. Just when he had worked himself up to his self-righteous best, he would let it slip that he himself had committed the very sin he had been warning them about. Caught in his own hypocrisy, he always offered only one excuse, the one the TV audience just knew was coming: "The devil made me do it!"

We all laughed, of course, because each of us saw ourselves in his silly skits. We're all looking for a devil to blame.

To be sure, there *is* a devil, and demons, too, alive

and active in this world—enemies of God and enemies of ours also. And it's true: we Christians are unwittingly being played all the time by these very subtle, supernatural, evil forces hoping to derail our lives. But let's drop the "devil made me do it" excuse. Because if the Spirit of the living God lives in us, Satan and his hosts may be able to blow in our ear, whisper their lies, and tempt us to doubt—but they cannot *make* believers sin.

Then, of course, there's *the world* and all the opportunities it offers to tempt us to sin and distract us from obeying God.

> *For everything in the world—the lust of the flesh, the lust of the eyes and the pride of life—comes not from the Father but from the world. (1 John 2:16)*

The world is anything that lures your heart away from God. But *the world* isn't only "out there." Any version of Christianity that offers a religious alternative to actually believing in and behaving like Jesus is also *the world*.

However, the other voice I hear most often isn't Satan's or the world's. It's my own; it's *me* resisting Jesus' full claim on my life as Lord. I've told him a thousand times he's my Lord and I've promised to love him and obey him. I meant it, and I still mean it! But there's an independent, sinful part of me that wants to reserve a part of my life for *me*. I want to be able to call at least part of my life *mine*.

The Apostle Paul said it well:

The moment I decide to do good, sin is there to trip me up. I truly delight in God's commands, but it's pretty obvious that not all of me joins in that delight. Parts of me covertly rebel, and just when I least expect it, they take charge. (Romans 7:21–23, MSG)

So, let's give it a name—call it *partial surrender*. And I've noticed that others who believe themselves to be Christians apparently have bought into the partial surrender idea, too; they like hanging on to their "mines" also. And there have been times I've begun believing the lie I so desperately wanted to believe—that because of grace, Jesus is fine with partial surrender.

Is he?

Is grace—the amazing truth that God through Christ Jesus has forgiven all our sins—really a contributing factor to my spiritual mediocrity?

It is, only when I abuse it.

Grace abuse is holding God to his promises while using them as an excuse to break our promises to him. Most of us wouldn't think of ourselves as actually doing that—but isn't that what we're really doing?

Christ's sacrifice was meant to pay the price for that which I *cannot* do for myself—perfection and absolute surrender. Jesus expects all of us who claim his name to full-heartedly give our all to loving God, doing his will, and serving his kingdom on earth. When that's not enough—and it isn't, of course—yes, in the end he remains faithful, even if we aren't. That's the real purpose of grace—to do what I can't. It should never be my excuse for what I won't.

So the primary reason some of us aren't making more progress on living more godly lives is that we've made peace with our consciences. We've come to what we think is a reasonable balance between sin and surrender—a compromise we can live with, and one we think God is okay with, too. We tell ourselves that Jesus died not just for our past sins but for our present and future ones as well. We've been forgiven! And that's a powerful incentive to settle for partial surrender. For *good enough.* Anything more just feels unnecessary—overkill.

But then you've just got to wonder what Jesus himself thinks when he hears us singing our hearts out in worship, "I surrender all," knowing full well that we have no real intention of surrendering all? And, "take my silver and my gold, not a mite would I withhold," when he's looking at millions of mites' worth of cars right out there in the parking lot! Who are we kidding? Singing songs we really don't mean and other thoughtless forms of worship simply perpetuates the illusion of surrender.

Is it really any wonder so many kids, gagging on this hypocrisy, are running for the church door when they finally leave home? Jesus himself might be right behind them if he weren't a million times more faithful to us than we are to him.

Grace.

I've often wondered if Jesus ever rubs his thumbs

slowly over the scars on his palms in disbelief that we would treat so casually his great love and terrible sacrifice.

So most of us try to obey that first voice, the *good* voice—what I believe is the Holy Spirit's voice—often enough to assuage our guilt and enable us to feel reasonably good about ourselves. And maybe you're doing about as well as most of your Christian friends or the people at church. But, deep down, you know that there has to be more—that your Savior and Lord deserves so much more *and wants* so much more for you!

Whoever pursues righteousness and love finds life, prosperity and honor. (Proverbs 21:21)

Disobedience Training

A short time after I was introduced to the Rule, it dawned on me why I wasn't making more progress in obedience. When I would feel a prompting of the Holy Spirit to do something I was reasonably certain Jesus wanted me to do—and then choose *not* to do it—I was actually rewarding myself for being disobedient.

I knew perfectly well that obedience would cost me something, at least in the short run: time, money, embarrassment, inconvenience, or pleasure deferred—you name it. If I choose *not* to obey Jesus, I can avoid all that grief and keep what is *mine*.

Sure, obedience results in rewards later in heaven, but I'm not always swayed by that promise. Sounds too much like delayed gratification to me. So I'm back to doing the moral math, desperately crunching the numbers again, this time on the cost/benefit ratio of obedience. If I obey, what's the impact on *me—right now*?

We can sniff out trouble a mile away—can't we? For sure, making ourselves available to Jesus 24–7 is going to wreak havoc with our hopes for a tidy Christian life.

The youth pastor in my church recently told me about a young Christian, new to town, who could use some guidance. Even before he finished talking, in my head I was counting the cost. Did I have time to meet with one more guy regularly? He also mentioned that the student he wanted me to meet didn't have a car. Not only did that mean more driving for me, I also knew myself well enough to know that I'd feel guilty that I had so much while he had so little. Would I find myself having to raise money for a car for him?

My mind raced through the calculations, counting the cost way beyond the youth pastor's simple request to have a cup of coffee with a stranger. It still amazes me how creative I am at thinking up reasons to not obey God. Maybe I'm so good at it because I've had so much practice.

I had to consciously stop myself and think about the 10-Second Rule: *Clare, don't worry about where this might lead, don't overthink it—just do the next thing you're reasonably certain Jesus wants you to do.*

It turned out that the young guy was amazing. We've met many times since. I almost missed a God-appointed relationship in my frenzied attempt to protect *myself, my* time, *my* money—*mine, mine, mine.*

Do I always spend time logically comparing the pros and cons of each decision every time I have a spirit-like impression to do something good, then make a willful choice to disobey? No. But here's the painful truth about bad habits: Almost without thinking, we usually choose the least costly or least painful path. It's part of our sinful nature. And if I do it often enough, disobedience will become, or will continue to be, second nature to me.

Why do I have this natural impulse to not obey? Because almost everything Jesus taught is counterintuitive, that is, it *goes against our natural instincts*. Our natural instinct is self-preservation—preservation of our status, our lifestyles, our options, our time, our space, and our rights. *I have rights!*

But do we? Do we really? Jesus said we must consciously deny ourselves, which includes denying ourselves whatever rights we think we have, and choose to live a life of self-expenditure.

Then he said to them all: "Whoever wants to be my disciple must deny themselves and take up their cross daily and follow me. For whoever wants to save his life will lose it, but whoever loses their life for me will save it." (Luke 9:23–24)

But what does "take up their cross daily" actually mean? Hold on—because what I'm about to tell you is going to sound contradictory to what I said only a few pages back regarding surrender. *I gave up on absolute surrender years ago!*

I gave it up because I realized it was an impossible goal. I knew there was no way I could ever hope to absolutely surrender my will to God's will perfectly, every day, for the rest of my life. God knows it. And every other Christian on earth does, too, whether they'll admit it or not. And none of us wants to chase a dream or a goal we know can't ever be attained. As a result and without any conscious decision on our part, most of us have given up pursuing the impossible and have resigned ourselves to a more *pragmatic Christianity*, the spirituality of our Christian friends rather than Jesus. I've personally found that it's a lot easier to be like them than to be like *him*. *We can do that!*

So, how do we break free from that *good enough* mind-set and dare dream of pursuing the *impossible* again? Here's how: Even though absolute surrender is impossible, doing the next thing I'm reasonably certain Jesus wants me to do *isn't!* I *can* do that! And so can you.

Therefore, the second foundational principle that

makes the Rule work is this: *The Rule gives you a place to begin again following Jesus, right now and whenever you find yourself drifting spiritually.*

Even knowing you'll never surrender *all*, living by the Rule is a way to begin surrendering *more!*

Remember when Jesus said in Matthew 6 not to worry about tomorrow, for tomorrow will take care of itself? It's as if Jesus is saying to you and me, "Just start here today; trust me." When you and I give up trying to figure it all out ahead of time and simply follow Jesus, daily and hourly and in the next ten seconds, doing whatever he asks us to do, we'll actually move closer to that previously elusive ideal of absolute surrender than we ever dreamed possible. That's exactly what dying (surrendering) daily to the will of God, means.

It's following Jesus made simple!

Not everyone who says to me, "Lord, Lord," will enter the kingdom of heaven, but only he who does the will of my Father who is in heaven.

—MATTHEW 7:21

CHAPTER THREE

Listening to the
Voice of God

Listen for God's voice in everything you do, everywhere you go;
he's the one who will keep you on track.

—PROVERBS 3:6, MSG

So, here's a question you have to be asking yourself about now (I know I did!): "Before I begin following Jesus in simple, spontaneous obedience, how do I know these *voices*, these impressions I'm sensing are, in fact, from him?"

To begin with, I prefer words like *impression* or *sensed* when describing this voice. Frankly, I get a little nervous when people tell me, declaratively, "God told me to . . ." That's possible, of course, but I just wouldn't personally dare stamp *thus saith the Lord* on anything, with absolute certainty, outside of Scripture.

Perhaps that's because I've never actually heard an audible voice from God. Some have. I haven't. There are many stories in Scripture about men and women who heard audibly from God or heard Jesus speak. I used to long for God to speak to me with that clarity, until one day it dawned on me that he has. Twenty-first-century Christians have something no one mentioned in the Bible had—the whole Bible! In it, God speaks to us from every page.

So when I use words like *impression* or *voice*, I'm not referring to an actual, audible voice. It's more like a thought that arrives with a strong feeling that it's coming from one of the Trinity. It immediately feels right and true. These impressions often remind me of something I learned from Scripture: a story, a proverb, a parable, a command. And always—*always*—they're consistent with what the Bible teaches and with godly character.

In John 10, Jesus said that the watchman's sheep *"follow him because they know his voice. But they will never follow a stranger; in fact, they will run away from him because they do not recognize a stranger's voice. . . . I am the good shepherd. I know my sheep and my sheep know me"* (verses 4–5, 14). How, then, can we be reasonably certain we're hearing the true shepherd's voice?

While it's true that God also communicates to us through creation, music, godly counsel, and preaching, Christians have always accepted Scripture as our ultimate authority for spiritual and moral truth.

My son, if you accept my words and store up my commands within you, turning your ear to wisdom and applying your heart to understanding—indeed, if you call out for insight and cry aloud for understanding, and if you look for it as for silver and search for it as for hidden treasure, then you will understand the fear of the LORD and find the knowledge of God. (Proverbs 2:1–5)

The third foundational principle of the Rule, and perhaps the most important one of all, is this: *The more you know about the teachings and character of Jesus Christ, the more confident you'll become following him.*

Therefore, chapter 9, "The School of Jesus," is devoted almost entirely to helping you become so familiar with the teachings and habits of Jesus that in these everyday promptings of the Holy Spirit you can know with growing confidence just how you ought to respond in most situations. *"I have set you an example that you should do as I have done for you"* (John 13:15). But here's a sneak preview of how these stories about Jesus give him a *voice* beyond his quoted teachings and commands to us.

When I was a child, if one of my friends had said, "Your mother told me she wants you to help the next person you meet who needs it," I would have believed them. Given my mother's character, and how I've seen her treat people all her life, that sounds like something she'd do herself—and, therefore, like something she might ask of me. I wouldn't have had to personally *hear* her voice to confirm my friend's message. *Her life was her voice.* So it is with Jesus' life.

Jesus' followers recognize his voice because they've studied his words and his life so intently they've developed a spiritual ear for God.

The Bible provides us with some examples of how God moves in people to act without hearing an actual voice.

Luke reports in chapter 2, verse 27, that Simeon, a righteous and devoted man, was "moved by the Spirit" to go to the temple to see baby Jesus.

In Acts 15, Paul and Barnabas came from Antioch to Jerusalem because other church leaders had been telling new Gentile converts that, in order to be saved, they needed to be circumcised and obey the Law of Moses. Paul disagreed with that, so the Council of Jerusalem decided to meet, pray, and talk it through. There's no indication in Scripture that the Holy Spirit spoke audibly to them. Nevertheless, they were able to come to a conclusion and act on it, framing it in these terms: *"It seemed good to the Holy Spirit and to us"* (Acts 15:28). Apparently they sensed, or had an impression, that the Holy Spirit was guiding them to act in a specific way.

Many of my responses to these impressions feel like that to me—*they seem good to the Holy Spirit, and they seem good to me.*

Standing Orders vs. Special Instructions

The Holy Spirit speaks to us for a variety of specific purposes. The impressions you and I receive from God generally fall into three broad categories:

> **REMINDERS**. These impressions are like a green light reminding us of what God has said we must do, or ought to do, as taught in Scripture (a *thou shalt*).

> **WARNINGS**. These impressions are like a warning buzzer, reminding us of a sin we've already committed or we're contemplating—something that God has said is either wrong or very unwise (a *thou shalt not*).

> **SPECIAL INSTRUCTIONS**. These impressions may take different forms. In some Christian traditions it could include the spiritual gifts of prophecy or tongues. However, the ones we're most concerned with here are like an instant message, giving us specific guidance as to whom we ought to serve, and how, at a given moment.

The first two kinds of impressions—*reminders* and *warnings*—are simply reminders from God of commands that we ought to have learned from the Bible. There shouldn't be uncertainty, for instance, over whether or not we should lie, steal, be unkind, or be unfaithful to our spouses.

You may have sensed these warnings the last time you were about to sign your tax return or submit your expense or mileage report. Or just before you press "Send" after having composed an email in anger or to someone with whom you should never be corresponding. *Danger ahead!*

Likewise, we shouldn't be standing around thinking that, unless God specifically reminds us to be kind and generous, we don't have to be. So when God, speaking through Paul in Colossians 3:12, says, *"Therefore, as God's chosen people, holy and dearly loved, clothe yourselves with compassion, kindness, humility, gentleness and patience,"* his words aren't just wishful thinking. He expects all who call themselves his followers to live like that, 24–7.

In military terms, these positive and negative commands or admonitions are our *standing orders*. These standing orders aren't new, they've been clearly stated in Scripture for centuries. Nor are they special instructions to you personally and only—all Christians are expected to obey them. And we don't get a bye just because other Christians seem to be ignoring them, or are tempting us to violate them.

One night I was having a conversation with a woman who was reluctant to forgive her husband for an offense, even though he had apologized profusely and shown true repentance for what he'd done. "I'm waiting for God to tell me when to forgive him," she said.

"I think God's already done that," I said. "When Jesus told his disciples to forgive seventy times seven, it wasn't something he was asking them to pray about. He expected them—as he now expects us—to do it."

The woman then told me that she had been open to forgiving her husband for some time, but several friends had urged her *not* to—a message she was susceptible to, since she was still so hurt.

"If you listened to God, rather than to your friends— what is *he* telling you to do?" I asked, and her face softened. She knew what she had to do. And she did.

You'd think those of us who've been Christians for a while wouldn't really need the Holy Spirit reminding us of these standing orders. We ought to know better by now. However, it's been my experience that because of sin, I too am prone to moral amnesia when it suits me, especially when *my rights* are threatened.

So, just as our children occasionally had to be reminded of our instructions or warned before they made a poor choice, the Holy Spirit often does the same for the children of God. This is exactly what Jesus promised the Holy Spirit would do for us: *"convict . . . in regard to sin and righteousness"* and *"guide you into all truth"* (John 16:8–13, NIV 1984).

Most of the impressions I personally believe I'm receiving from God are simply reminders of these universal, standing orders of God, which I know I ought to always obey, but still resist far too often.

Special Instructions

Special instructions, on the other hand, are new orders—orders calling us to do something not specifically commanded in Scripture, such as helping a particular person at a particular time. They are *not* special revelations of new truth from God. These instructions to do something out of the ordinary will never violate God's moral laws or any teachings of Scripture; instead, they will encourage you to apply those laws or teachings in some specific way for the good of others or the kingdom of God.

It may be something as simple as being impressed by God to trade places in a long line with an older person, or sensing Jesus asking you to turn off the game you're watching, go into the kitchen, and give your wife a hug for no reason whatsoever. It could also be inviting a boy without an engaged, spiritual father to go fishing with you or stopping whatever you're doing right then to thank God for some small blessing from him. Will it be clear *why* God asked you to follow each particular instruction? Sometimes. At other times, we may be asked to follow him in ways we can't, and perhaps never will, fully understand.

A young businessman I mentored was traveling alone. One night he sat on the edge of his hotel bed, locked in a spiritual battle—and losing. In his hand was a remote, and in front of him a big-screen TV. With a few quick clicks, he could be transported to a world he had visited too many times before—the world of pornography.

He knew he had a problem, and he also knew that he needed to fight it. Earlier that evening, faced with the temptation of the hotel-room TV, he had gone for a walk in the parking lot, praying for the strength to resist. But throughout his walk, *the voice* almost hissed; serpent-like, "One more time won't kill you. You're a Christian; God will forgive you. Come on! You deserve a little reward." Now, back in his room, he was ready for that *reward*.

His ringing cell phone startled him. *It's 10:15 at night—who'd be calling me now?* He picked up the phone, saw that the call was from me, and answered.

Just moments before I had felt a prompting to call and encourage him. All I knew, though, was that he was traveling and that he hated the loneliness of the road. I *didn't* know that he struggled with pornography, because he'd been too ashamed to tell me.

When he heard me launch into a message of encouragement and affirmation, he broke down, and for a short time he could barely speak. Then it all came gushing out. A lifetime of sexual fantasies, pornography—even clubs. He poured out his heart, and I just listened and let him unload. When the flood petered out, we spoke, and he agreed to meet regularly with some godly men who themselves have been set free from this addictive sin.

Out of all the people God put on my mind that day, how did I know to take the extra step of calling him—and just him? That's what we're going to talk about next.

How Can We Be Certain?

Can I say with certainty that every impression I believe I'm getting from God, actually is? No! I suspect that, this side of heaven, there will always be a degree of uncertainty in our ability to discern God's voice. And don't let the fact that we have some seriously goofy Christians who occasionally make headlines with their outrageous claims "directly from God" turn you off to the reality that the Holy Spirit does communicate with believers. The Bible isn't clear as to exactly how the Holy Spirit does that, but this we know—*he does,* or there's no real point in praying for guidance or wisdom for situations that aren't clearly prescribed in the Bible.

Part of our problem is that Jesus didn't give us specific instructions on choosing which broken-down cars we should stop for, or a five-item checklist to consult before we decide to call a friend he's put on our mind. It's the ambiguity of these "special instruction" impressions that most confuses us. And when we're not sure, we tend to play it safe—and do nothing.

I've also known good people who've been reluctant to respond to these impressions for fear of being out of the perfect will of God. Yes, I believe God does have a perfect will for our lives, but obeying him daily may just be how God leads us to it. The men and women I've known whose lives are characterized by this simple but courageous childlike obedience end up making career, college, ministry, and marriage choices with far less angst, precisely because they spent far more time actually *doing* the will of God than *looking* for it.

So, here's the fourth principle of the Rule that makes following Jesus work in real life: *The Rule doesn't* require that you be absolutely certain an impression is from God before you obey. To be reasonably certain enough to act on an impulse or impression from God, you only need to believe it's the kind of thing Jesus himself might do if he were you. In fact, the need for certainty is often the enemy of obedience.

The psalmist said, *"I have considered my ways and have turned my steps to your statutes. I will hasten and not delay to obey your commands"* (Psalm 119:59–60). When we obey God spontaneously and immediately, love trumps logic most of the time.

I've been asked if I've ever misread the will of God when following one of these impressions? "Probably thousands of times" is my honest answer, "but I'm not certain I would ever know it, even if I did."

Christians have somehow gotten the notion that if we respond and things turn out the way we expect—then it must have been the will of God. On the other hand, if it turns out differently—a failure, in our opinion—it *must not* have been the will of God.

Really? I wouldn't put it past God to let me fail occasionally, if only to humble me or to teach me to be more dependent on him in some way. If he tested Abraham with his instructions to sacrifice Isaac (Genesis 22), why wouldn't he test us?

Even so, think about it. Let's just say that an impression you felt wasn't really from God. What's the worst that can happen? You've still done something kind and good for someone, or you've kept yourself from doing something you know you shouldn't. How can that *not* be the will of God?

It's in these special instruction situations that I find my adult sensibilities don't always serve me well. If I were a little child, I would just do it. Perhaps that's one of the reasons Jesus implored us in Mark 10 to have the faith of children. Spontaneous obedience has a childish feel to it. But once you get past the adult obsession with certainty, it's freeing!

A Warning About "Buts"

The next time you have an impression from God to do something out of your comfort zone, listen for the *but*. *But,* God, I don't . . . *But,* Jesus, I just can't . . . Here's the danger with *buts* to the life of a true follower of Jesus.

Almost every time a person uses the word *but* in an ordinary conversation between two people, what the speaker is really saying is this: "The importance of what I'm about to tell you is my reason, or excuse, for not taking more seriously what you just told me." Isn't that true? It almost always negates whatever statement came before the word *but*.

So, my wife, Susan, tells me, "You rarely do the romantic things you used to do when we were first married." Then I respond, "*But* look at all the other great things I do for you." (Sound familiar?) My *buts* to the promptings of God aren't received any better by him than they are by my wife.

When God impresses you to do something and you hear yourself respond mentally with a *but,* be very careful. That word and the thought that follows it are very likely the *other voice*.

Using the Rule with Wisdom

Some decisions in life are so serious and have such major implications for ourselves and others that we need to take time to carefully and prayerfully listen to God. *I wouldn't advise using the 10-Second Rule to make any momentous decisions: whom you will marry, what job you ought to take, whether to serve in leadership, make a major investment, or adopt a child. You'll need time, prayer, godly counsel, and wisdom before making serious decisions such as those.*

The 10-Second Rule is best reserved for resisting everyday temptations and for acting on godlike impressions to be kind, encouraging, and generous. In other words, for "entry-level obedience."

There are some exceptions. It may be that you've been struggling with an addiction, or you're in a relationship you know is wrong, or you have a habitual sin you've been wrestling with for years, or you're bitter and unforgiving toward someone who has wounded you deeply, or you've been resisting Jesus' call to surrender your life to him. The next time God impresses you to put off your old self and make that kind of decision, one you've known for a long time he's been wanting you to make, do it immediately!

You were taught, with regard to your former way of life, to put off your old self, which is being corrupted by its deceitful desires; to be made new in the attitude of your minds; and to put on the new self, created to be like God in true righteousness and holiness. (Ephesians 4:22–24)

Waiting for a Sign?

There are biblical accounts of people testing the will of God using signs, however, those were apparently rare even then, and they certainly aren't the normal way God directs his people today. He most often spoke to them, as he does to us, through prayer, fasting, Scripture, and counsel of godly men and women. Think about it; asking for a big dramatic sign before you move out in simple obedience doesn't really require faith at all. It's literally walking by sight—*not by faith!*

Nevertheless, we Christians still like the idea of signs, don't we? Perhaps that's because it puts the responsibility back on God before we have to act. And, it seems like we don't need much in the way of signs from God to do what we *want to do*. A vague, almost unnoticeable twitch on the face of God will do the trick—any sign will do. No, the way I've seen the "waiting for a sign" system used most often is for direction regarding something we would secretly prefer *not doing.*

Ken Davis, a Christian comedian, tells a humorous story of a Christian who gets on an empty city bus, walks to the rear, and sits down. *Lord,* he prays, *if you want me to speak to someone about you, please give me a sign.* At the next stop another passenger gets on, goes all the way to the back of the bus, and sits right down next to the Christian. "Do you know anything about Jesus?" the passenger asks.

The Christian excuses himself for a moment and slowly bows his head once again and prays,

> *Lord, if you really want me to talk to this stranger, I need just one more sign. Please turn the bus driver into an armadillo.*

Have you been praying for armadillos?

Have you been waiting for a sign from God you really hope never comes before getting serious about following him, or have you been playing it safe, taking your cues from your friends rather than Christ?

I've imagined this scene in my head: I'm playing baseball with Jesus. The stands are full of fans, but out there on the field it's just him and me. I'm the pitcher. Jesus is the catcher, behind home plate. He settles into his crouch, ready to play, and I look for his signals—simple commands. What pitch will he want me to throw? I wait in anticipation, but also with one eye on the crowd. What will they think of me?

He signals a fastball.

I think for a moment and shake my head—no, not a fastball.

Next he signals a slider.

This time I look toward my teammates in the dugout for guidance. Then I glance up at the fans. No, I'm not comfortable with that one either.

He gives me yet a third signal.

No, not today, thank you!

Then I imagine Jesus silently and slowly withdrawing his signaling hand back into his mitt. There's a deep disappointment in his eyes. He's decided to let me throw whatever I want. So I do—and then I wonder why there's just no team spirit anymore!

Has Jesus stopped giving you signals?

I doubt it. He never stops speaking to his children. Is there a signal God's been trying to give you, even as you read this sentence, that you're ignoring because you just don't want to obey?

Anyone, then, who knows the good he ought to do and doesn't do it, sins.

—JAMES 4:17, NIV 1984

CHAPTER FOUR

Why Your Simple Obedience Matters

For we are God's handiwork,
created in Christ Jesus to do good works,
which God prepared in advance for us to do.

    —EPHESIANS 2:10

'm a history buff. World War II, in particular, fascinates me because of the clarity of the cause: good versus evil. I'm equally fascinated by its scope—almost the entire world engaged in this terrible death match for freedom.

Watching the film *Saving Private Ryan* one evening, I was drawn to the scene where the Allied troops are landing on the beaches at Normandy, France. As the men jumped off their landing crafts into the water, with bullets flying everywhere, wading ashore through the floating corpses of their comrades, I tried to imagine the fears, doubts, and questions those incredible men must have been wrestling with at that moment.

They had to have been asking themselves: *Is risking my life really going to make any difference? With tens of millions of people fighting all over the world, will my individual contribution, perhaps even my death, really matter? Is this cause really worth my life?*

With the benefit of history and from the safety of my armchair, I may presume to answer: Yes, it was worth it! We live free today because of the obedience and bravery, even unto death, of every single soldier, and of the millions of equally committed men and women all over the world who were more devoted to the greater good of mankind than to their own lives. Yes, their individual sacrifices mattered.

And so does yours.

It would dishonor the men and women who served in World War II to compare their blood sacrifice with the inconveniences we experience following the

10-Second Rule, but there are some similarities. One of the reasons you and I are often reluctant to follow Jesus is that it's hard to see how our small life truly fits into the eternal plans of God. Does my obedience—my sacrifice—really matter to the larger cause?

It's my hope that by the end of this chapter, you'll have a fresh perspective on why your simple obedience in small things like the Rule does matter to God, to every person you know and, like those brave soldiers, to people you might never know.

You're More Than a Christian

The day you came to faith and were born again, you became part of the most powerful family in all of history—the family of God! *"Yet to all who received him, to those who believed in his name, he gave the right to become children of God—children born not of natural descent, nor of human decision or a husband's will, but born of God"* (John 1:12–13).

God the Father became *our* father, Jesus became *our* elder brother, and every true follower of Jesus, man, woman, and child, became your spiritual family and mine. We have this in common: identical spiritual DNA. I used to think this family talk was just a metaphor, but I was wrong. *"Whoever does God's will is my brother and sister and mother,"* Jesus said in Mark 3:35. And *"you are no longer foreigners and strangers, but fellow citizens with God's people and also members of God's household,"* we are told in Ephesians 2:19.

That's why you're not "just a Christian," or just a member of First Baptist or Lincoln Assembly of God. As a member of God's family, your mission in life is to be Jesus' stand-in. That means he expects you to behave like him—as if he lived in your house, raised your children, saw the same strangers and needy people you see, and hung out with your friends. More than that—it's intentionally living with your spiritual radar full on, eagerly anticipating his next assignment.

When Jesus instructed his disciples to pray *"May your kingdom come. May your will be done on earth as it is in heaven,"* it wasn't just wishful thinking on Jesus' part about his future kingdom. He actually expects his followers, his brothers and sisters, to bring the kingdom to earth—that is, to act on his behalf in *your* world.

Environmentalists have a saying, "Think globally—act locally." The kingdom of God and the eternal purposes of God, like the idea of absolute surrender, are so big it's tough to get our minds around them. But we can do this: We can live out the Rule *locally*—in front of the people we live with and meet every day, consistently enough to change *the world* around us.

When our children were small, they had chores. They weren't always happy about their assignments, but they did them. As kids, they couldn't possibly understand how their thousands of simple acts of obedience contributed to the orderly management of our large household. Neither could they have imagined at the time that in doing them they were actually learning the skills of cooperation and self-sacrifice so important for their own future households, vocations, and relationships.

There's a reason Jesus asks us to do these "divine chores" in the family of God. As spiritual children, simple obedience to his requests like the Rule gets things done in the household of faith, or the kingdom of God, that we can't possibly understand now or maybe ever.

The Boy at the Bus Stop

I first saw the boy standing on a snow bank at a bus stop, wearing only a light Windbreaker on a very cold day. At eighteen or nineteen, with his back to the driving snow, he looked as thin and frail as a sparrow. That morning I had spoken at a local high school about the 10-Second Rule. Wouldn't you know it? As soon as I saw him, I had the impression that I ought to stop and offer him a ride. I have to confess, my first thought was to get to my next appointment. But I rolled down the window and made the offer. To my relief, he needed to go only about six miles, right on my way.

Within a few minutes, he was relaxed enough to begin talking about his life—and a tough life it had been.

He'd left his home, in a small town in another state, where his family was a mess. He'd been in our town only a few months and had tried a few churches, including mine, more out of loneliness than out of a search for God.

He told me he wasn't a Christian yet, so we talked about that for the few minutes we had together. "I'd like to send you some information on what the Bible says about Jesus, and I'd enjoy having a cup of coffee or lunch sometime with you," I said. I gave him my name and cell phone number. I got his address and sent him the material I'd promised, along with a simple explanation of the gospel and a Bible. I never heard from him again.

People have asked me if I considered that a failure. Not at all. My only responsibility was to do the next thing I was reasonably certain Jesus wanted me to do. I don't know whether I was the first real Christian he'd ever talked to, or maybe the second to the last, just before he made a commitment to Jesus. Or maybe he's still spiritually lost.

Here's the point: Most of the time we're going to be clueless as to why God asks us to do these little *chores* for him. I'd love it if I were always able to understand his endgame. Perhaps God has four, or six, or who knows how many of these 10-Second Rule encounters planned for this young man, all requiring faithful Christians to play their part in the salvation of this one person.

Would I have loved it if he had called and I'd had the privilege of personally introducing him to Jesus? Of course! But apparently my only task was to be faithful to the impression God gave me. That was the will of God for me that day—at that moment.

Maybe God has assigned *you* to meet him next.

I know, O LORD, that people's lives are not their own; it is not for them to direct their steps. (Jeremiah 10:23)

God's Secrets

It's almost a cliché to say God has a purpose and plan for all things. But it's true—he does. And we've been given a glimpse, in Scripture, of how it will all turn out in the end. But how he orchestrates our lives from day to day to pull it all off is largely unknown and unknowable, except to God himself.

Society refers to the nice things people do for others as "random acts of kindness." However, God is anything but random. He's sovereign over this world of his, and everything he absolutely wants done, gets done. God isn't wringing his hands with angst, hoping like mad we do what he wants, otherwise *his will* just won't get done. God doesn't need us to do anything—but he expects us to do everything.

So, no impression that's truly from God is ever random. Through our simple, faithful obedience, combined with the obedience of our spiritual family members all over the world, he's putting together a puzzle that he alone sees in its entirety, piece by piece.

> *The secret things belong to the LORD our God, but the things revealed belong to us and to our children forever, that we may follow all the words of this law. (Deuteronomy 29:29)*

As his children, it's rare that we're ever privileged to see the whole chain reaction our obedience sets off in the lives of others, or theirs in ours. Nor does God expect us to understand the big picture. To risk another cliché, Jesus simply expects us to trust and obey.

My mother passed along to our family the story of her godly grandmother who, during the Depression, felt that God was calling her to care for a neighbor woman and her children the next farm over who were sick with tuberculosis, then a deadly disease, so that her husband could bring in the desperately needed harvest.

My great-grandmother and her husband prayed about it and decided that, if Jesus told us to love our neighbor, then she really had no choice but to care for them. So for months she courageously devoted herself to them. Miraculously, the neighbor woman and her family fully recovered. However, my great-grandmother caught the disease, and when she returned to her own family, she gave it to two of her children. All three of them died.

Our first reaction to a story like this is, "What a tragedy!"

I don't think God sees it that way. Who but God himself knows how the children of the family that lived turned out? Did they go on to live virtuous and faithful lives, blessing even more people? I have no idea. One could ask, "What about those who died—what might they have done had they lived?" Was this just one more senseless death or the plan of God for some greater good? We can't really know, and this is where the rubber meets the road. Even if we don't understand, can we really trust God "to work out all things for the good of those who love him?" (My paraphrase of Romans 8:28.) The secret things of God are best left to God. Trust and obey.

I've often wondered how many hundreds or thousands of small, selfless, Christlike decisions one has to make to get to the point where we're willing to lay down our life for another as my great-grandmother did.

That's really what the Rule is all about—it's the recalibration of our character, one obedience click at a time, slowly conforming us to the image of Christ as we trust that he has a reason beyond our understanding.

That's true faith!

Training Ourselves to Be Godly

The fifth and last foundational and transformational principle that gives flesh to following Jesus via the Rule is this: *Christian character is shaped less by your big, dramatic decisions than by the cumulative impact of thousands of small acts of simple obedience.* Those small acts shape our character and prepare our hearts to accept even more bold assignments from God. They are the building blocks for a life that God truly blesses.

Godliness is both the result *and* the reward of these mini battles, fought and won dozens of times each day to resist sin and look for ways to make life better for others. It's *there*, in these small skirmishes with the *other voice*, that our true character, good or bad, is slowly forged.

> *Consider it pure joy, my brothers, whenever you face trials of many kinds, because you know that the testing of your faith develops perseverance. Perseverance must finish its work so that you may be mature and complete, not lacking anything. (James 1:2–4)*

The purpose of obeying the 10-Second Rule is to help us develop these habits of obedience, beginning with the small things. Like Bill Murray's hypochondriac character in the movie *What About Bob?*, significant change takes place one baby step at a time. That's how we develop good habits. It's also how we break bad ones.

Frankly, I'm a couch potato. But if I were serious about running in the Boston Marathon, and it wasn't just wishful thinking, I would start small. A half mile the first day or two, adding mileage and speed with every week. For the first week or two, every morning, my body would scream: *Who cares if you're in the marathon? Give yourself a break today. Sleep in!* But I would know if I stayed with it, each day it would get easier. I'd get stronger, and so would the habit of regular exercise.

Reading this book won't make you obedient, any more than reading a book on running will make you a runner. There's only one way to become obedient, and that's to obey!

Practice. Practice. Practice.

That's exactly what Paul is telling Timothy, his apprentice, about the spiritual life in 1 Timothy 4:7–8: *"Train yourself to be godly. For physical training is of some value, but godliness has value for all things, holding promise for both the present life and the life to come."*

We're seriously delusional if we think we're going to be faithful when Jesus calls us to some big thing if we haven't put in the miles by training ourselves daily and preparing our hearts and our wills to eagerly anticipate the crack of the starter's pistol.

Living in the Zone

Long-distance runners and other athletes talk about being in *the zone*. It's that mental place you arrive at after tremendous exertion that energizes you to go even further, that place where most of the pain stops, hope returns, and you know you can finish the race.

When you and I live out the will of God with passion, the Holy Spirit enables us to find *the zone*. It's that place where self-sacrifice no longer feels like duty, and the joy of being in the will of God drowns out most thoughts of the cost. *"And the peace of God, which transcends all understanding, will guard your hearts and your minds in Christ Jesus"* (Philippians 4:7).

When millions of us get that intentional about imitating Christ, the kingdom family will explode! The 10-Second Rule is more than just a clever memory device to help us tweak our obedience skills some. It's one of the primary ways God's will gets done on earth as it is in heaven: by following Jesus' directions day and night—imitating him.

In our day heaven and earth are on tiptoe waiting for the emerging of a Spirit-led, Spirit-empowered people. All of creation watches expectantly for the springing up of a disciplined, freely gathered, martyr people who know in this life the life and power of the kingdom of God. It has happened before. It can happen again.*

—RICHARD FOSTER

---

*Richard Foster, *Celebration of Discipline* (San Francisco, Harper & Row, 1978), p. 150.

The Five Foundational Principles
of the 10-Second Rule

1. When you're reasonably certain Jesus is asking you to do something—do it immediately! (Procrastination is not your friend.)

2. The Rule gives you a place to begin again following Jesus, right now and whenever you find yourself drifting spiritually.

3. The more you know about the teachings and character of Jesus Christ, the more confident you'll become following him.

4. The Rule doesn't require that you be absolutely certain an impression is from God before you obey. (The need for certainty is often the enemy of obedience.)

5. Christian character is shaped less by your big, dramatic decisions than by the cumulative impact of thousands of small acts of simple obedience.

PART II

THE PRACTICES

CHAPTER FIVE

The Power of Small Beginnings

He sees in your heart the understandable yearning
for comfort and conformity; the plans, the savings,
the predictable wish list of a tidy life. But he also sees
in your soul the thirst for adventure.

—PETE GREIG, THE VISION AND THE VOW

One beautiful, sunny, crisp winter's day when our children were small, we went to a park on the edge of a large lake. The kids wanted to play on the ice. Uncertain whether the ice was thick enough to be safe, I asked them to wait until I tested it by gently stepping onto the ice closest to shore.

My three little girls covered their faces with their

mittened hands, sure their dad was about to drop out of sight. After my first few tentative steps, when the ice seemed to hold, I began sliding my feet slowly across the icy surface. After shuffling twenty feet or so, I tried taking full steps. Finally, fully confident in the ice's strength, I entertained my children by dancing a little jig and invited them to join me on the ice for games. They thought I was the bravest man on earth. I was their hero, and I loved every minute of it!

Later, sitting on the park bench watching them play, I had an epiphany. Clearly I was a cautious dad—but I was also a cautious Christian, just beginning my faith journey. I was considering making what for me were some very bold faith decisions—and up until then, my faith had seldom really been tested. What was holding me back from growing as a new follower of Jesus was my lack of confidence that my faith, like the ice on that lake, would really hold. Theologically, I believed that God could do anything. But *would* he? I believed it—but I hadn't yet put it to the test.

Ice-Testing Time

On that park bench that day, the Holy Spirit spoke to me with a strong prompting to put aside my doubts and begin "testing the ice"—testing God with baby steps of obedience. He brought to my mind a portion of this verse I had memorized as a child: *"The one who is in you is greater than the one who is in the world"* (1 John 4:4).

This was twenty years before I'd ever heard of the 10-Second Rule. But on that day I began observing the spirit of it, nonetheless. I waited for God to speak to me, or to provide opportunities that would have scared the wits out of me only weeks before. And when those opportunities arose, in the raw jargon of a novice follower, I threw my brains out the window and simply obeyed.

Many of those opportunities that came my way were ones I'd rather have passed on. For example, shortly afterward, a friend asked me to attend a men's Bible study at a restaurant. *In public.* To make matters worse, it was at a restaurant where I'd been meeting my friends for years for coffee, gossip, and dirty jokes. The voice—that second voice, the one that accuses—was pulling out all the stops that first morning: "You hypocrite! You self-righteous . . . you, you, you . . ."

But I took a deep breath, said a prayer, and walked through that restaurant, waving sheepishly at my friends there for coffee and gossip, trying to look both cool and spiritual. I carried my Bible down low, close to my leg, trying to keep it out of sight. *What's wrong with this picture?* I wondered. I'd been a Christian all my life—gone to Christian schools, church every Sunday—and yet that morning I'd have been more comfortable walking through that restaurant carrying a case of bras.

But God used that study not only to teach me more about the Bible, but to help me learn simple obedience in the face of doubt and fear of failure.

Only a few months into that study, another friend asked, "Would you like to go to an evangelism seminar with me?" *No, I really wouldn't,* was my immediate thought. I didn't need to be a brain surgeon to figure out that once I went to that seminar, I'd actually be expected to talk to people about Jesus.

The irony was that I was a talker. I could talk all

day long about my church, family, business—almost everything. But to actually sit down one-on-one with another person who, I assumed, wouldn't want to buy what I was selling and share my faith; I couldn't imagine that. But apparently Jesus could. So I quietly said yes before I changed my mind.

Remember, that's the first powerful principle behind the 10-Second Rule. When you're reasonably certain Jesus is asking you to do something, *do it immediately!* Waiting just gives you a chance to overthink these impressions of God, providing fertile soil for disobedience, making it just that much easier to say no to God again the next time he speaks.

To my surprise, God used that evangelism seminar to embolden me to be his agent of grace to other men in my life. It became habitual: God would bring names to my mind, and I would call, meet them for lunch, and share the spiritual journey I was on. Then I would listen to see how they responded.

Did it always go well? No. I'm sure some men thought I'd lost my mind. Instead, what I began losing was my fear—because if I'm doing what I'm reasonably certain Jesus wants me to do, what is there to fear? I felt like I was flying without a net and loving it!

The point of these stories is that I had to start somewhere. And I'll be forever grateful to God for allowing me the freedom to trust him with my infant faith until I was able to take bigger steps.

> *I tell you the truth, if you have faith as small as a mustard seed, you can say to this mountain, "Move from here to there" and it will move. Nothing will be impossible for you. (Matthew 17:20–21)*

Developing Trust in God

I'm not sure why it's so difficult to trust God. It's what we generally do when all else fails, when all other options have been exhausted. There's even a joke about a church leader who once cried out in exasperation, "Prayer! Has it come to that?"

There are many things we might fear when our faith is being tested, and one of them, for sure, is this: If we put our full weight on God, and our attempt fails, will it lay bare doubts that have always lingered at the fringes of our hearts? Doubts such as: Maybe I'm not really saved at all. And if I decide to live boldly and fail, will that be the final evidence that proves to me that I don't really belong to God? Where will that leave me? Can I risk it?

Or doubts even darker: Is it possible that *none of this is true*? Perhaps there really is no God, or I have the wrong God, or the Jews have it right and Jesus wasn't God.

Tell me you've never had such thoughts, even momentarily.

One of my doubts is even less spiritual: I'm afraid of looking foolish. *Did you hear about Clare? He wrote a book. He thinks God impressed him to write it. Yeah, right. I guess we'll see if that "impressions from God" stuff really works!*

I admit it—there have been times I've not done what I was reasonably certain Jesus wanted me to do because I've been more afraid of the opinions of others than of failing God.

For they loved human praise more than praise from God. (John 12:43)

Is there something you're reasonably certain God has been impressing you to do for your own spiritual growth, but fear or pride is holding you back? The Rule isn't only about helping others. Has a friend recently asked you to attend a Bible study? Has your wife asked you to begin praying with her? Have you sensed God urging you to read the Bible daily yourself?

More important, are you not yet a true follower of Jesus? Have you sensed Jesus calling you to abandon yourself to faith alone in him?

Maybe it's ice-testing time for you, too.

Learning to Be Faithful in Small Things

Whoever can be trusted with very little can also be trusted with much, and whoever is dishonest with very little will also be dishonest with much. (Luke 16:10)

Therefore consider carefully how you listen. Whoever has will be given more; whoever does not have, even what he thinks he has will be taken from him. (Luke 8:18)

If you are faithful in small things, Jesus was telling us in those passages, *you will be entrusted with even greater things.*

But the inverse of that statement is also true: *If you are not faithful in the little things, you will not be entrusted with greater things.* Perhaps God has some larger purpose in mind for you, but he wants first to test and shape your character. Do you really want his will and his glory, or yours?

Let's be honest. Okay, I'll go first. I don't daydream about being faithful in small things. I'm ashamed how often I hope people notice the *big* things I'm doing for God and admire me for it. Even as I was writing this book, I'm embarrassed to admit I had moments when I imagined standing before a crowd, humbly explaining how this unworthy servant came to write what *Christianity Today* would name the Book of the Year. (They haven't, of course—not yet.)

How about you—do you, too, have fame fantasies?

Singing to a stadium full of fans or a church packed with worshippers, tears running down their faces at the sound of your voice. Scoring the winning goal. Showing up at your high school reunion thin, rich, and beautiful. Or maybe yours are on a more spiritual level: being honored by your pastor from the pulpit for your leadership, or as an example of humble servanthood the whole church ought to emulate.

Why do we have these daydreams?

Because it's far easier to dream of glory than doing whatever it takes to achieve the dream—especially in the spiritual realm. And most of the hard work it takes to build a life that truly pleases God usually goes unnoticed by nearly everyone—except God. If only there was a way to attain a Christlike reputation for humility, holiness, and self-sacrifice without having to develop it so slowly and largely in obscurity. If I ever wrote *The Lazy Man's Guide to Spiritual Greatness,* I'd be a millionaire—and a fraud.

A friend of mine flies a lot—enough to get upgraded to first class often. It's more than the extra legroom and better service that he likes. He's honest enough to admit that he feels superior and pampered in first class. People notice him.

He was on a trip a few years ago, sitting in the terminal waiting for his call to board—*first,* of course—when he notices an older, poorly dressed woman in a wheelchair, and as he tells it, "Wouldn't you know it! I had a 10-Second Rule moment!"

He went over to the woman and asked her where she was sitting on the plane. Obviously she was a little surprised by his question and reluctant to respond, so he just came out with it. "Hi, my name is Josh. I'm sitting in first class and if you're in economy, I'd be honored if you would take my boarding pass, and let me take yours. You look like you could use the extra room."

"Why would you do that?" she asked, even more anxious that this was some kind of scam or a trick.

"I'm trying to obey the 10-Second Rule," he said, "which says just do the next thing you're reasonably certain Jesus wants you to do. A few minutes ago God gave me the thought to exchange seats with you. So, is it a deal?"

He knew it was when she broke out with a smile that lit up her face. And when she admitted that she'd never flown first class in her entire life, tears came—to both of them.

After telling me this story, he went on to admit the experience also brought out a dark side of him. "I knew I had done the right thing, but I missed the attention I got in first class." Even worse, he actually fantasized the flight attendant in first class getting on the intercom and thanking "Mr. Peterson sitting way back in seat 99F, who generously traded his first class seat with Mrs. Smith, who otherwise would have been sitting with most of you, back in our cattle car. Let's all give Mr. Peterson a hand. What a saint!"

Right at that moment, sitting in his seat, he realized just how desperately he needed to die more to self. The holy grail for him has become learning to serve others in the little things, even when nobody but God and the person he helped knows what he's done. Many dream of doing great things for God, half hoping he won't ask. Fewer wake each day longing to be used by him—*that* day.

No one who really wants to count for God can afford to play at Christianity.

—H. A. IRONSIDE

CHAPTER SIX

Pre-decisions

Everyone thinks of changing humanity and nobody thinks of changing themselves.

—LEO TOLSTOY

T he ragged, unshaven, middle-aged man stood at a busy intersection in the bone-chilling wind of a very cold winter, holding a cardboard sign. I'M UNEMPLOYED. CAN YOU HELP? was scrawled in black marker.

The minute I saw him, my guilt meter went off like a five-alarm fire. But this was more than thirty years ago, when I was driven more by guilt and pride than by God. (Too often, I probably still am.)

Our small children were in the backseat, accompanying Dad on his Saturday morning chores after a fun breakfast—a typical Saturday morning. The light turned red as we approached the intersection, which meant that, of course, we stopped smack-dab next to this guy. Rather than thinking of how I should respond, I began racing through my reservoir of reasons why I actually shouldn't.

If he's strong enough to stand there all day, why doesn't he get a job? How can I possibly know if his needs are legit or not? He's probably gotten help from sixteen other people already this morning. In those days, I usually scanned the faces of panhandlers for those telltale signs of alcoholism—a few red veins on the nose was often enough to disqualify them. But most of the time I just tried hard not to look them in the eyes so that I might not accidentally humanize them.

"Dad, why don't we give him some money?" one of the kids asked.

I was about to give my children a little sermonette on responsibility and stewardship when it dawned on me that I was sitting in a $25,000 car, warm, overfed from the breakfast I hadn't even finished, and was now running errands to buy stuff we really didn't need. The absurdity of the self-righteous answers I was about to give compared to this man's simple request for a few dollars I didn't really need, embarrassed me.

So we stopped and gave him some money. Genuine compassion? Not really. I probably did it more out of my desire to look good to my kids. But it made me think: *Why is it I felt so unprepared for these pop quizzes God occasionally sent my way?*

Living Intentionally

I love the word *intentional*. It helps me draw a clearer distinction between a theoretical openness to follow Jesus and a carefully thought-out decision to obey.

One of the best ways I know to overcome indecision and prepare myself to obey Jesus more intentionally, in addition to Scripture and prayer, is to make what a friend of mine calls a *pre-decision*. Simply put, it's using these times of failure, these times when we've been caught flat-footed, as an occasion to learn—and to formulate a specific plan of action for next time. *There will be a next time!*

There's an old joke in Christian circles: "Do you know how to make God laugh? Tell him your five-year plan." I've added this twist: "Do you know how to make God cry? Tell him you have no plan."

My father had a friend who owed him a good deal of money, a man who went to our church. John drove a nice car and took expensive vacations but never seemed to have enough left over to repay my father. No interest, nothing on the principal—nothing!

One day my father came back to the office where we worked together, laughing as he came up the walk. I knew he'd been meeting with the guy I thought of as a deadbeat. Was it possible he'd finally gotten paid? "Why the smiles, Dad?" I asked, giving him an opening to tell me every juicy morsel of the story before he showed me the check.

"I just saw John," he said. "That guy has more brass than a ship! When I pressed him for a payment, he looked me straight in the eye and in dead earnest said, 'Gord, just trust me—you *will* get paid. I'd rather owe it to you all my life than ever cheat you out of it!'"

You see, John believed himself to be a man of integrity because he had some vague notion of repaying my father sometime, somehow. Just not today. And my father somehow found that humorous. I didn't.

I don't think God finds our lack of intentionality funny either.

A family therapist once gave me this wise advice when I was reluctant to change something I was doing: "If nothing changes, nothing changes." Meaning that unless I have thoughtfully and prayerfully considered how I ought to live and act differently, I'm likely to make the very same mistakes again next time.

Pre-decisions in Real Life

I was in Chicago on North Michigan Avenue a few years ago, and I saw one of the hundreds of homeless men I've seen many times. God gave me an impulse to stop and talk to one particular man and offer to have lunch with him. My heart wasn't really in it. Even after more than ten years of living the Rule, I still groan a bit when I sense God taking me out of my comfort zone.

But by this time I'd already made some pre-decisions about dealing with homeless men, if and when God moved me to do so: If I was alone or with only one of my children or an older grandchild, and I felt urged by

God to do so, I'd try to buy them a meal. So I asked, "Are you hungry? Let me buy you lunch."

"Yeah, sure," the man said without enthusiasm. I was sure he was hungry, so I just figured that he was as wary of me as I used to be of guys like him. This was new territory for both of us.

Despite his initial misgivings, he ate like he was going to the chair!

Between mouthfuls, he asked an obvious question: "Why does a guy like you want to have lunch with a guy like me?" Somewhat sheepishly I answered, "To be honest, I didn't. But I'm a follower of Jesus, and I'm trying to obey the 10-Second Rule."

By the way, I've found that nobody can leave that statement alone. Almost every time, they'll ask what the 10-Second Rule is. It has been an amazing way to begin some wonderful conversations about Jesus. Predictably, he asked, I answered, and then we had a nice talk about his life, his dreams, where he'd gone wrong, his scattered and fractured family—all kinds of things.

Was I any real help to him? I don't know. But I left that restaurant a better man than I'd been when I had

entered. Like most people, I often thought of homeless panhandlers as simply a nuisance rather than as real
human beings with crushed dreams. God may have in-
tended that one encounter, on that day, only for *me*—to
soften my heart.

Learning to Be Kind More Wisely

On that day in Chicago I gave a meal and my time.
Other times, I've been impressed to give homeless or
out-of-work people small amounts of money. People
have questioned me: "Aren't you concerned that they'll
just waste that money on alcohol or drugs, hurting
themselves?"

It's a good point, and over the years I've learned
greater wisdom in these situations. I rarely give much
cash these days. In fact, I'm occasionally impressed by
God *not* to give money, but that's probably more for me
than them. Not giving money forces me to invest more
of myself in people instead, even if only briefly.

Now when I see men with NEED WORK signs and
I'm impressed by God to stop, rather than simply throw-
ing money at the problem to erase my guilt or because

it's the quickest solution, I'll often ask what they really need right now. If it's food, I'll drive them to get what they need and try to steer them toward nutritious food. I generally offer to take them and their groceries to wherever they live. (Those of us who have transportation sometimes forget to think about how people we might help will actually get this stuff home.)

If it's truly a job they need, and if I have one, I've offered temporary work to some, even if only for a few hours. I also keep small New Testaments in my trunk. Others I know have made pre-decisions to keep food cards for local stores in their glove compartments. My wife keeps warm socks and blankets in her car. Others keep fleece sweaters. (In Michigan, it gets cold.)

Another reason I don't give much cash anymore is that I don't want my help to be a source of temptation, if in fact they do have a drug or alcohol problem. But that shouldn't be my excuse for withholding either help or encouragement in some way.

Do not withhold good from those who deserve it, when it is in your power to act. (Proverbs 3:27, NIV 1984)

The truth is, I'm far more likely to waste money than they are. Do you have any idea how much of God's money I waste every day on lattes, movies, vacations, clothes, eating out? I just tend not to think of it as waste when I spend it on myself or my family. And I suspect that I'm not the only one.

Let's face it: If we're really going to be serious about waste, we ought to start with ourselves. I'm nearly certain Jesus would prefer that I "waste money" on a poor person, if I do it wisely, than on myself.

Pre-decisions for Personal Holiness

When I first began doing the Rule and thinking about pre-decisions, I almost invariably thought of them in terms of doing something kind or generous for others. However, I find pre-decisions just as helpful in the area of personal holiness. Nobody can possibly anticipate the thousands of special-instruction impressions God might ask of us, so we cannot make pre-decisions that address all of them. But each of us knows only too well the list of our own private sins. We can prepare ourselves for facing them.

Years ago I heard a guest on the *Focus on the Family* radio broadcast suggest this pre-decision idea for your teenagers: Rather than going to church one Sunday morning, take some personal time for this one assignment: *Spend an hour or two alone with God, seek his guidance, and then make a mental list, strictly between God and yourself, of the things you'll never do, or never do again.*

The power of a pre-decision like that is obvious. *Now* is the time for them to think through the temptations they're going to face someday, not when they're out with friends, or on a hot date with a new love. Hopefully, at some point, when they know they're getting close to violating the boundary they've pre-decided not to cross, the Holy Spirit will cause them to remember a decision made months or even years before.

A pre-decision won't stop them (or us) if we're flat-out determined to give ourselves over to passion or pressure. But it still serves a purpose—it's a speed bump to warn us that we're about to go over the cliff.

This exercise works as well for adults as it does for teenagers. Take an hour or two—this week—and make a list of your own "nevers."

One woman who did this exercise was almost immediately convicted that her choices of magazines, books, and TV shows she watched were sending terribly conflicting signals to her children. She had always taught them to be discerning about what they watched, but she wasn't doing the same herself. *Do as I say, not as I do.* Courageously, she made a list of shows and reading material she would never again watch or read, and she showed it to her kids and told them why. By doing so, not only was she being intentional about holiness, but it was a great example to her children of how pre-decisions work in real life.

A college student once told me she's made some pre-decisions for what she'll do the next time she's at the movies or watching a DVD with friends and she's convicted that this is no film for a follower of Jesus. Following through on her pre-decision will take courage, but she's wise enough to know that vague, good intentions alone, without a plan, rarely work.

Last year I spoke at a men's retreat about the 10-Second Rule. I asked the men, "How many of you have sensed God impressing you strongly and often to be more pure in your sexual thought life, particularly the temptations you face when you travel or that your computer offers?"

Instantly, almost every hand in the room went up.

My next question: "How many of you have a specific plan to deal with that temptation?"

Fewer than half the hands went up this time. It saddened me, and I think it did God also, to think that, in all likelihood, more than half of those men will fail their next Holy Spirit warning simply because they haven't made any pre-decisions to do anything different the next time they face temptation.

If you're a man and have a "friend" who struggles with sexual temptation, you can go to our website and view *Personal Boundaries for Men*. It may help him out.

I have a theory as to why we're so unintentional about dealing with habitual sins. Really, it's not that hard to figure out: Secretly, we don't want to give up our pet sins. You know—the sins or bad habits we're not sure we can live without, or believe we could ever really be happy again if we did. Our pet sins give us a temporary release from the realities and stresses of life.

They comfort us. And we know full well that if we devise a real plan to deal with them, it means we're committing ourselves to have a serious go at it, or risk even greater feelings of guilt. So we often chose to put up with this dog that bites, rather than shoot our companion.

But here's the problem with compromise—*it's contagious.* Because I think I'm getting away with certain sins, I find I'm tempted even more in other areas. Perhaps you've had the same experience. Unless I'm intentional about personal holiness, it's amazing how quickly my pet sins give birth to others—especially those I once swore would never again get the better of me.

> *But each one is tempted when, by his own evil desire, he is dragged away and enticed. Then, after desire has conceived, it gives birth to sin; and sin, when it is full-grown, gives birth to death. (James 1:14–15)*

Habitual sins are both predicatable and preventable. So, the dog needs to die—and today, not tomorrow after just one last time in your lap.

In my experience, no matter how serious I am at doing good, habitual sins are like weights on a runner. The race can be run, but not well.

> *Therefore, since we are surrounded by such a great cloud of witnesses, let us throw off everything that hinders and the sin that so easily entangles, and let us run with perseverance the race marked out for us. (Hebrews 12:1)*

Tongue Control

I urge men to make pre-decisions to eradicate certain statements from their vocabulary that wound their wives like "You're just like your mother" or "You always . . ." (Actually, not making *any* statement that begins with "you" is a great pre-decision to guard against hurtful comments when tensions are high.) Women, you, too, know what words wound the man in your life.

We usually know, don't we, when we're about to use language unwisely: An unkind word is forming in our minds, or we're about to explode at our children or at the person in the car ahead of us. Everyone within earshot is about to get a lesson, good or bad, in how a child of God behaves.

What's your plan for the next time you find yourself at that ragged edge?

One woman I know admitted that she was convicted to make a pre-decision when she determined that she was speaking disrespectfully about her own mother in front of her children. She would not let that sin get the better of her again. Another man emailed me that he made some pre-decisions about his rough language and dirty jokes used thoughtlessly on the construction site after a new guy from work showed up at his church one Sunday. It was only then that he realized what a terrible witness he'd been on the job.

Here's another way I've learned to use the Rule: I listen for God's warnings more often now before I open my mouth. And for good reason. I have a great sense of humor. I love to laugh. I laugh at myself and others. But I can go over the edge way too quickly with sarcasm in the guise of humor. I've cut some people deeply, and as a result I've learned to pray often and think deeply about what I need to do to keep the blade safely in its sheath.

The Rule has been equally helpful when a badly needed apology seems glued to the back of my mouth, or when a prideful statement or a little white lie is shaping itself, spring-loaded and ready to impress someone with how spiritual I am, or to cover up something I'd prefer to keep secret.

I often hear warnings from the Holy Spirit when I'm on my way to meet with someone, anticipating a difficult conversation, and I'm already lining up my arguments, talking myself into an anger way beyond the importance of the issue. Sometimes it's only the Rule and a pre-decision on the fly that keeps me from embarrassing both God and myself—probably hurting someone else who doesn't deserve it.

Finally, brothers, whatever is true, whatever is noble, whatever is right, whatever is pure, whatever is lovely, whatever is admirable—if anything is excellent or praiseworthy—think about such things. (Philippians 4:8)

Failure—a Catalyst for Pre-decisions

The young woman, a junior in high school, could see some of her friends already gathered at the end of the hall in a tight circle, speaking softly, before she even arrived. They were gossiping about someone.

She could always tell. Their eyes betrayed them. If you're going to talk about someone in public, behind their back, you have to be constantly on the lookout for the victim. Eyes darting back and forth like radar is a dead giveaway. Someone's reputation was going down.

She was relieved for a moment. It wasn't about her. If she'd been the victim, the crowd would have melted away, suddenly remembering classes they had to get to. She didn't join in the feeding frenzy; she rarely did. But as she stood there, she sensed God wanted her to speak up—say *something* to stop this. But she didn't. She was afraid.

The way she told me the story, that afternoon at

home she sensed God speaking to her again: *Don't just confess your failure. Prepare for the next time. There will be a next time.*

So she took the time to read what the Bible had to say about gossip. She did some research online and read about how others have handled it. She learned that gossip isn't telling a lie. A story may very well be true. But gossip is truth inappropriately passed on—it just isn't necessary that anyone else know everything. She ran a few ideas past her youth pastor. Eventually, she felt that she knew the mind of Christ on this issue.

The "next time" didn't happen for a few weeks, but when it did, she now had the courage to speak out. She gently asked her friends, "Are we really being fair to Lisa by talking about her this way?" That simple question turned a toxic conversation on its head. A few girls thanked her later. Others said she was being self-righteous—but not to her face, of course.

Our married daughter, Megan, passed on this story at MeganVos.blogspot.com shortly after I began writing this book. It illustrates just how God can use even procrastination or failure to teach us that he's the God of second chances.

Our daughter was in a doctor's office sitting across from a woman who looked incredibly sad. The kind of sad that says, *I give up. I have nothing left.* Megan immediately sensed God nudging her to tell this total stranger that she was going to be okay. That's when the battle began.

This was a psychiatrist's office and, in Megan's words, "was probably filled with all kinds of looney people like myself. My hands began to shake and I felt panicky, so I didn't say anything, and before I knew it, she was out the door. Gone."

But then remembering the Rule, the Holy Spirit renewed her courage to act. So, she quickly left the office and found the woman waiting for the elevator and simply told her Jesus' message of encouragement. "I have absolutely no idea what you're going through, but I sensed God telling me to tell you that you're going to be okay." It was awkward being this reluctant prophet on the fly. Nevertheless, she did what God had impressed her to do even though she's sure it was more like ten minutes than ten seconds.

As a result, Megan has begun praying both for this stranger and herself. She prays that the woman *is* all right and that she thanks God for making her so. For herself, she's praying for the courage to act more boldly next time when God instructs her. She's sure there will be a next time, and she wants to be ready.

Later, reflecting on this experience, Megan had this wonderful insight. "I hate it when I have to ask my kids to do something a million times before they do it. And I'm sorry, but I do that to God all the time. *All the time!*"

That's our daughter. As flawed as her father and as transparent as plate glass.

The girl with the gossip dilemma, my daughter, and many others have learned this important lesson about the Rule: Even when you fail to follow the Rule at first, the discipline of the Rule causes you to ask important questions. "Why didn't I handle that better, or act immediately?" You'll learn something about yourself and about the subtle nature of procrastination: it is really just another form of self-deception.

So, a pre-decision is an intentional choice to learn

from these mistakes and consider a more Christlike response for the next time. And there *will* be a next time!

Pre-decisions are simply God's wisdom applied to real life.

> *If any of you lacks wisdom, he should ask God, who gives generously to all without finding fault, and it will be given to him.*
>
> —JAMES 1:5

CHAPTER SEVEN

Love the One You're With

In the morning we cannot yet know who our neighbor will be that day.[*]

—DALLAS WILLARD

borrowed the title for this chapter from a Stephen Stills song, popular forty years ago, but that's the only thing our two messages have in common. Here's mine: As you begin living by the Rule, how do you learn to love the people you're with, those you'll be called upon to help, who may not be all that lovable?

---

[*]Dallas Willard, *The Divine Conspiracy*, (San Francisco: Harper SanFrancisco, 1998), p. 111.

The tenth chapter of Luke, starting in verse 25, tells about the day a group of religious leaders came to Jesus, hoping to trip him up. One of them asked, "Teacher, what must I do to inherit eternal life?"

Jesus answered, "What is written in the Law?"

The man answered, "Love the Lord your God with all your heart and with all your soul and with all your strength and with all your mind; and, 'Love your neighbor as yourself.'" But after Jesus had affirmed that the man had answered correctly, the man asked, "And who is my neighbor?" This much is for sure—in asking this question, the man wasn't looking to expand his neighbor base.

Jesus answered by telling the story of the Good Samaritan.

It's a story we all know. In fact, one of the problems with this story is that it's too familiar. Even non-Christians know what the Good Samaritan did—he cared for a perfect stranger who had been mugged and left for dead after two other religious leaders had refused to get involved.

Because it's so familiar, we don't spend much time

thinking about the subtleties of that story and its implications for whom and how we serve. For instance, how many of us have noticed that the story never tells us whether the Good Samaritan loved or even liked the man he rescued? Although it's never clearly spelled out, the implication in the story is that the Samaritan didn't know the injured man—and yet he was compassionate enough to do something incredibly kind, at considerable personal expense and inconvenience, without knowing whether the victim was a good guy or a jerk.

As I began living by the Rule more and more consistently, my heart began raising all kinds of questions. I found myself getting anxious or angry over some of the people I was serving.

I was once ripped off by someone who claimed to be a Nigerian seminary student, standing in the back of church looking for and finding his next mark. And I've been taken advantage of more than once, even by people with legitimate needs who keep needing more. More money, more time, more whatever—just more. You'll learn over time to establish some boundaries, but you'll also find it helpful to come to terms with this truth: The risk-averse will rarely follow Jesus. Being taken advantage of occasionally is the occupational hazard of a servant.

> *"If someone takes unfair advantage of you, use the occasion to practice the servant life . . . Live generously."* (Luke 6:30, MSG)

Still, I've always found it easier to help people I like—good people who've just had a tough break. And I'm afraid the judge in me has often sorted people into these camps: *worthy* and *less worthy*. Or: *grateful* and *ungrateful*.

While I don't want to enable bad behavior, I realized over time that if I didn't have a change of attitude, I risked becoming jaded and cautious. I've known too many good-hearted people who've become disillusioned with obedience simply because it was just so hard, or they felt unappreciated. I didn't want that happening to me.

Serving Those Who Don't Deserve It

I began by searching the Gospels, trying to find a single person Jesus deemed undeserving of grace. About the only people I found for whom Jesus had no patience or grace were religious hypocrites trying to justify themselves, which, I realized with embarrassment, was exactly what I was doing when I resisted helping someone I didn't like, and yet I still claimed to follow Jesus! Even the woman caught in adultery and the cheating tax collector Zacchaeus found kindness and forgiveness from Jesus.

In practical terms, what did that mean for me? Do I really need to stop for every homeless or out-of-work person holding a sign? No—but it does mean I can't disqualify them from grace simply because I think they don't deserve it. If Jesus didn't, I guess I can't either.

Many years ago, I started spending time regularly with Jim, a very lonely guy who can be extremely difficult at times. We still meet regularly. At times he can be quiet and gentle, then, in the next moment, demanding and selfish. Why do I keep meeting with him? Perhaps it's just the optimist in me that wants to believe real transformation is just around the corner—hope. I'd also like to think love is my motive. But it could be as simple and self-serving as wanting a few guys like Jim on my résumé when I finally see Jesus someday, to cover my failures. Who knows? It's complicated.

Once after sharing a meal with our family, I dropped him back at the group home where he lives. As we pulled away on our way back home, my son, sitting in the backseat, was uncharacteristically quiet. Finally he asked, "Dad, do you really like Jim?"

"Not yet," I said.

Here's the point: I don't always like everyone I'm called upon to serve. And unfortunately, I've discovered I can't make myself enjoy someone I don't. God can do that in me, but through no act of my will or psychological technique can I create in myself heartfelt love and admiration for another human being. There's a Christian book titled *Love Is a Choice*. I believe that it is. And I've decided that I'm okay with that. Loving your neighbors means being kind and gracious to people you may not like—until you do. Maybe.

Victims or Perpetrators

I used to have another moral sorting mechanism. I separated people into two groups: first, victims of other people and circumstances beyond their control; and second, those who appeared to have shot themselves in the foot. Surely Jesus would favor victims!

But in the story of the sheep and the goats in Matthew 25, Jesus makes no distinction between visiting prisoners who are innocent or those who are truly guilty, between going to the hospital to visit a person injured by a drunk driver and visiting the drunk who's dying of cirrhosis of the liver.

However they got broken, lonely, hopeless, poor, or jailed, for whatever reason, Jesus seems to move them to the head of the line and then says to us, "Care for them—and I'll tell you why someday."

And when we do . . .

The King will reply, "Truly I tell you, whatever you did for one of the least of these brothers and sisters of mine, you did for me." (Matthew 25:40)

Loving the *Fringe People* in Your Life

I recently heard about a woman who, when her heart is prompted, makes a point of thanking or complimenting service people—busboys, hotel maids, cooks, baristas—those people at the fringes of our lives, largely unnoticed and unappreciated. When God nudges her, she'll immediately get up, walk across the room, and tell them how appreciative she is for how hard they work, or their cheerfulness, or whatever it was that caught her attention.

After observing the Rule for only a few months, a friend of mine discovered that he also has the spiritual gift of encouragement. He'll write a note to anyone as soon as God inspires him to. In fact, because he's made a pre-decision to be faithful and proactive in this, he now carries note cards in his briefcase and in his car. He leaves his notes with harried airline personnel, faithful church staff, and people he meets who appear to be having a tough day. When I get his notes, somehow they mean more to me than an email. Because he had to take time to write the note by hand, address an envelope, and mail it, they make me feel valued. In fact, I keep a file full of notes that friend and others have written me that I pull out on days when I wish someone would hide all sharp objects.

Kindness is cheap. It costs so little and yields so much, it's a shock we don't use it more often. It's an oil that heals the discouraged and lubricates any relationship from a marriage to a chance interaction with a stranger.

A few years ago I did a seminar at a local church. While I was setting up, a woman approached me, introduced herself, and said, "I just want to thank you for saving my life."

I thought I hadn't heard her correctly. I couldn't recall ever seeing her before, so I immediately stopped what I was doing and asked her to explain.

"You wouldn't remember me," she said, "but I remember you. Last year my life was such a mess, I was seriously contemplating suicide. So I asked God for a sign—anything, any sign that I should change my mind. I went to a Denny's restaurant that morning. As I was walking in, you opened the door for me and said, 'I hope you have a good day.' That was it—my sign. I realized it immediately. And it saved my life. Thank you." She hugged me and walked off.

I don't tell this story to impress you with how faithful I am. I'm certain that I've failed to say something kind or cheerful to thousands of people over the years. I tell the story just to illustrate the truth that you and I have absolutely no idea how powerful simple acts of kindness and encouragement can be in the lives of people who may be hanging by a thread.

Learning Even from Disappointment and Failure

A person emailed this story to me: While sitting in church listening to a sermon about honoring your father and mother, he felt a strong impression from God to call his father—a man who, frankly, still frightens him. He got up immediately, walked out on the half-finished sermon, called his father, and simply told him that he'd been prompted by God to thank him for all the ways he'd provided for him while he was growing up.

The son has dreamt of the day his father would tearfully assure him that he loved him. It wasn't to be this day. But when the son hung up and his heart stopped racing, he felt good. He had done the will of God.

When you live by the Rule, sometimes knowing

you've done the right thing will be your only reward. I've been deeply disappointed so many times by the apparent lack of gratitude from the people I've helped. In my imagination, I envision tears of gratitude, smiles of joy, trembling hands reaching out to shake mine. Apparently, it's still too much about me.

I received an email just last week from a guy I met only once. On that occasion, we briefly discussed the Rule. A few days later he was approached on the street by a homeless person. He immediately felt a prompting of God and enthusiastically opened his wallet—only to find that it held nothing but a single one-dollar bill. So he gave what he had.

The homeless man took it, stared at the lone bill for a moment, and then turned and walked away without a word.

My friend was angry all the way home—until he received the *next* impression from God: *That's what you do to me all the time. You rarely thank me for small blessings anymore.*

If God stopped loving us and providing for us because we didn't deserve it or appreciate it, we'd all be in trouble.

Here's another truth about me: I love to serve, but I resent being treated like a servant. As long as I can choose the time and nature of my service to others, I'm generally fine with it. But there's a side of me—my dark side—that still resists inconvenient assignments from God.

However, followers of Jesus ought to be wary of showing *measured mercy*—mercy that's portioned out only as time or convenience allows. We call that volunteering: a very good thing. But it's not the same as spontaneous obedience.

I've made what I thought were simple stops for broken-down cars. What do you do when it becomes apparent that the people you stopped to help don't have money for repairs or a tow? Or that they're strangers just passing through, with no money and no place to stay? When that happens to me, I confess, I silently groan— still trying to protect what's *mine*.

Think about this: If we truly mean it when we say "It all belongs to God," then when we give someone a gift of money, we're doing nothing less than passing on his dollars or checks to another person. We're actually carrying Jesus' wallet! If I'm not prepared to identify that closely with Jesus, I'm not sure I have the right to call myself a follower of his.

In the interest of full disclosure, it's not like I'm driving around looking for people in need all day. I may go out of my way to help total strangers in a significant way three or four times a month. I don't think about it that much anymore. I used to pat myself on the back when I did only because it was so rare.

When the Rule becomes second nature—when you find yourself praying for, preparing for, and anticipating how God will use you—when you begin looking for more "neighbors" to help in unique ways—then the Rule has progressed, for you, from a rule of life to a lifestyle.

CHAPTER EIGHT

From a Rule of Life to a Lifestyle

They love one another. They never fail to help widows;
they save orphans from those who would hurt them.
If they have something they give freely to the man who
has nothing; if they see a stranger they take them home,
and are happy, as though he were a real brother. They
don't consider themselves brothers in the usual sense,
but brothers instead through the Spirit, in God.

> —ARISTIDES' DESCRIPTION OF CHRISTIANS TO THE
> ROMAN EMPEROR HADRIAN

As Aristides observed in the quotation above, the early church took Jesus seriously. From the opening chapters of the book of Acts on, we read that, upon responding to the gospel, people began immediately loving God with wholehearted devotion. They took to heart Jesus' command to love others as much as they loved themselves.

In fact, the early church was so radical in its love and lifestyle that within a few centuries millions of people became followers of Jesus. The kingdom of God spread like wildfire—not because Christians had some grand plan or a carefully thought-out strategy, but because they simply followed Jesus' commands. The people around them found Jesus and this radical new love shown by his followers irresistible!

That's no longer an accurate description of Western Christianity. Too many adults still have a Sunday-school understanding of Jesus and his gospel that they've never outgrown. They heard the Bible stories of Jesus as children, and they still think of him primarily as a gentle lamb, brilliant teacher, and suffering Savior. And of course he was, and is.

But that imagery keeps us from thinking of Jesus as a revolutionary—calling his followers to a conspiracy of the faithful. Jesus declared open war on greed, injustice, anger, failure to forgive or love extravagantly, lust, poverty, religious hypocrisy—and on any and all beliefs, worldviews, or lifestyles other than those prescribed by God. Neither the American Revolution, nor the French Revolution, nor any of the recent upheavals in many Arab nations, is as radical as the revolution Jesus has enlisted us to: a revolution to change life on this planet as we know it, one life at a time. We're told to have childlike faith, but he didn't leave us with a childlike vision.

I'd like to introduce you to four people who have caught Christ's vision for this revolution in their own lives and are promoting the revolution to others. None of the four are saints—each has issues—but all have taken obedience to the next level. If we ever hope to win the admiration of our world as those first Christians did, the followers of Jesus will have to respond to God's Word and the leading of his Spirit as faithfully as these four.

Brad

My friend Brad has been more bold in living out the 10-Second Rule than almost anyone I know. When I first met him, Brad was a young, energetic leader in the making, organized, focused, and on a mission to build his business and net worth. What a salesman! This guy could have sold brass knuckles to Gandhi.

One day, over coffee, I shared with Brad the 10-Second Rule. He listened, but I could tell it wasn't getting much traction.

As he drove back to his office, he looked across the river winding through our town and spotted the veterans' home, looking as tired as the residents he imagined lived there. Immediately he felt a prompting from God to go there. He almost laughed out loud. *You're kidding, Lord! Not a building full of old, chain-smoking, sick guys. No way!*

But right on the heels of that terrible thought came another: *Could this be one of those 10-Second Rule things Clare talked about?* So he pulled off the freeway, parked his Lexus, and went in. He told the surprised receptionist, "I'd like to meet some of the veterans and encourage them. May I go in?"

Much to his relief, she told him he couldn't. He'd have to take a volunteer's class first.

Well, that's that, he thought. *I was obedient. Now I'm out of here.* But, immediately, he received another impression: that he was to sign up for the class. So he did, on the spot.

Soon afterward came the first of many afternoons that Brad spent sitting in the dayroom of the home, mostly just listening to these aging heroes: lonely old soldiers who told him the same stories they'd been telling each other for years. Stories of valor and honor, and also of families that seemed to have forgotten them. Stories of empty days and crushed dreams.

Brad noticed one veteran named Sam, a huge, surly man who, as a result of injuries presumably from the war, didn't have much face left. He usually sat alone. Brad tried to avoid him—no direct eye contact. Brad wasn't the only one; nobody seemed to like Sam.

One day after chapel, an orderly asked Brad to escort Sam back to his room. What Brad really wanted to do was run for the door. But, with as much grace as he could muster, he introduced himself to Sam and held out his arm for Sam to grasp. Walking was difficult for Sam, as it was for many of the veterans, and slowly, arm in arm, they made their way through the dingy hallways, which smelled of urine and disinfectant, back to Sam's room. Brad noticed a Bible on the small table by Sam's bed. "May I read you something from the Bible?" he asked. Brad then read Psalm 23 and quickly left.

Relieved to be out of there—out of the smells and into the bright sunshine—Brad slowly drew fresh air into his lungs as he walked to his car. But God had one more impression for Brad that day: *I want you to learn to be as comfortable around Sam as you are with your friends at the country club.* And with that, Brad had a sudden realization, one that moved him to tears. This whole exercise at the veterans' hospital had never been simply about him befriending old soldiers. God had something else in mind: breaking Brad's heart and teaching him to love and serve the least of these.

That's been my experience, too. In all likelihood, following the 10-Second Rule has benefited me more, by shaping my life in a godly direction, than it's helped those I've served.

Sometimes when I've been obedient and I'm feeling self-righteous and prideful about the wonderful things

I'm doing for people, God hits me upside the head. *You still don't get it! This exercise was for you! You needed this more than they did.*

> *Do nothing out of selfish ambition or vain conceit, but in humility consider others better than yourselves. Each of you should look not only to your own interest, but also to the interests of others. Your attitude should be the same as that of Christ Jesus: Who, being in very nature God, did not consider equality with God something to be grasped, but made himself nothing, taking the very nature of a servant, being made in human likeness. (Philippians 2:3–7)*

The Rest of the Story . . .

A few years back, Brad left behind his dream of material success to work full-time for half the money in a ministry teaching others to be more generous and obedient. In fact, he and his associates started a website, www .ilikegiving.com, to encourage generosity. Check it out.

Brad has more stories of doing the Rule than I do.

"Clare," he said, "at first it felt weird when I'd have an impression to call someone and simply tell them God had put their name on my mind and then ask them, 'How can I pray for you?' I'm sure some people felt uncomfortable. But a surprising number would initially get quiet and then start pouring out their fears and frustrations."

From surprising a young mother juggling two babies and heavy bags of groceries at a bus stop with money for a used car, to paying for the gas of a car that looked like it had coasted into the station on fumes, and in countless other situations, Brad and his wife have committed themselves to looking for opportunities to be *grace dispensers.* When the family goes out to eat, Mom and Dad often ask their children, "Who shall we bless today?" One or more of the family may notice an employee or even a customer and sense God telling them that this person needs encouragement. Sometimes that encouragement is a small gift, at other times simply a compliment.

As a family, they've chosen to ask God to give them radar for people's needs. They believe that if they actually expect God to speak, he will. They read the newspaper together and watch the news for stories of people whose lives are falling apart. Then, together, they pray about how, or whether, they ought to respond. This isn't simply about Mom and Dad being generous. The kids are expected to work to earn money for these family projects. Imagine how the habits of spontaneous generosity are being built into those children!

> *Train a child in the way he should go, and when he is old he will not turn from it. (Proverbs 22:6)*

Like all families, Brad's family isn't perfect. They're not the Waltons. But what started as an experiment doing the Rule has now become their lifestyle—it helps define who they are as a family. It's one of the unintended consequences of a surrendered life. They didn't set out to transform their lives. God transformed it, one obedient step at a time.

Susan and Veti

Years ago, my wife, Susan, was in Albania with a small group exploring the possibility of adoption and orphan care in that unbelievably poor country. Visiting the primitive children's hospital, where the medical care was vintage 1930s, her heart broke. Tearfully, she asked if there were any children whose lives could be saved if they had medical care in the United States. "Yes, we keep a list of children we've sent home to die who we believe could be saved."

It would take another whole book to explain how all this came about. For now, let's just say my courageous wife, Susan, in Albania for completely different reasons, obeyed the mother of all 10-Second Rules. Spontaneously, she offered to take two dying children from the list, children she'd never met, to the United States, where she thought they might have a chance at life, even if only a slim one. On top of it, she had only three days to make all the arrangements—passports, U.S. visas, medical records, airline tickets—while others informed their parents and got the children from the small villages where they lived and brought them to the airport. Everyone thought she was nuts—except God.

On the day Susan and the two girls assigned to her were to arrive in the United States, I had lunch with a friend, who was a fundraiser for the JESUS film.* When I told him what Susan was doing and how excited I was, he broke into a grin. "Clare, come out to my car with me; you're not going to believe this!" In the parking lot, he popped the trunk release. In the center of his spotless trunk was only one thing: a video of the JESUS film in Albanian!

"I cleaned out my trunk last Saturday," he said, "and I was about to throw the video out. I didn't need it any longer; we raised all the money we need. But I sensed God telling me, *Don't.* So I didn't. Now I know why. Here you go—it's yours."

When Susan and the children arrived in Grand Rapids, Michigan, things were chaotic. In the busyness of all the preparations for surgeries, finding food Albanians would eat, and lining up translators, all the while managing a family of seven, the video was temporarily forgotten. However, I had obtained several copies of the New Testament in Albanian, and Veti, the fifteen-year-old Albanian girl Susan had brought home, began devouring it, reading six or more hours a day for weeks.

---

*The JESUS film, Campus Crusade for Christ, 1979.

We could barely get her to take a break for meals. (Trust me, we never had that problem with our own kids!)

Seeds were being planted.

While Susan hurried off to the Chicago Children's Hospital with the other girl who needed immediate and very complicated, life-threatening heart surgery, I stayed home with our two youngest children and Veti, still recuperating from her surgery and treatment for advanced peritonitis and a botched colostomy. It was then that I finally got around to the *Jesus* film. One morning before I went to work, I showed Veti how to work the video player—no small task for someone who had never even turned on a TV weeks before. Fascinated, she began marathon viewings of the film, stunned to see this Jesus she had been reading about for the past few weeks actually come to life on the screen.

Raised Muslim, Veti had never heard the true story of Jesus. Now, here he was calling her to abandon all else: *"I love you—come follow me."* And she did. And she's been deeply in love with him ever since.

We returned both girls, now healthy, to their unbelievably grateful parents in Albania. However, one year later we invited Veti to return to the United States to live with us and attend high school and college here. In her nine years living in our home, her love for God was infectious.

Inspired by the fire they saw in both my wife and Veti, the faith community rallied, generously and spontaneously responding to the incredible needs Susan had seen in Albania. Hundreds of people who months before couldn't have found Albania on the map at gunpoint were transforming Albanian hospitals, building orphanages, and performing hundreds of operations. Awareness of God soared as the citizens of one of the most atheistic countries on earth saw Jesus in the faces of sweaty, smiling Americans who were also citizens of another kingdom.

Fast-forward eleven years. Susan and I are walking with Veti, by then a missionary to gypsies with Pioneers, a Christian missions agency. She'd been living in a cold, mountainous region of Kosovo, where Veti uses the Rule almost daily to receive Jesus' instructions on who to help, and how.

We watched with fascination and pride as barefooted women and children followed her like she was

Jesus through the filthy village. She brought them medical supplies, food, and children's evangelistic material. Daily, she was their advocate to get fair treatment and health care—just loving them because Jesus loves her!

Who could have imagined that out of one decision to listen to God's gentle voice and obey him, the lives of thousands of people would be affected? This is for sure: Susan, then Veti, then hundreds of volunteers, became linked together in this amazing chain reaction of grace that continues to this day.

Kyle

A half-dozen years ago, I took four high school seniors out West for a week of skiing and mentoring—teaching them to think like Jesus and helping them to develop a biblical worldview. The Rule was part of the drill, but I had no idea how far God was going to take that simple idea in the lives of some of them.

After the trip, one of the students, Kyle, sent an envelope stuffed with twenty-five twenty-dollar bills to the office of a local Christian high school. The note inside said,

Please let the entire student body know that any student can come to the office and get $20.00 to give to another person who needs it badly. My only request is that the student giving the $20.00 email me with what the need was, and the reaction of the person receiving it. I've set up a new email address for responses because I prefer to remain anonymous.

—A RECENT STUDENT AND FOLLOWER
OF JESUS

A curious parent emailed the anonymous donor with one question: "Why?" The response was simple: "This year I committed myself to live by the 10-Second Rule, and God recently impressed on me this idea to encourage generosity, so I did it. How it's all going to work is a little unclear to me, but I guess that's God's business."

Two years later, by then in college, Kyle (not his real name) hadn't stopped living by the Rule. As his faith grew more and more bold, he and another student from our trip out West were moved to help organize a cross-country bike ride that raised more than $60,000 to purchase special bikes for coffee farmers in Rwanda. When they started that effort, they hadn't a clue how to go about it—they just moved forward by faith. Once on the road, they often had no idea where they were even going to sleep that night. When they felt God was prompting them to do it, they would often ask total strangers for help. Characteristically, God provided kind and generous people to help them at nearly every stop.

Kyle—a straight-A student, a good-looking guy with leadership qualities from a well-connected family—has graduated now and is working with OneHope, a worldwide evangelistic ministry to children. He could have had any job he wanted straight out of college; he could be making tons of money. His life reminds me of what the writer of Hebrews in verse 12:1 admonished all of us to do: *"Let us throw off everything that hinders and the sin that so easily entangles. And let us run with perseverance the race marked out for us."*

Crediting the Rule for this young man's life would be like the rooster taking credit for the sunrise. He has godly parents and a circle of spiritual friends who have cheered him on all his life. The Rule simply served as a reminder to not overthink the impressions God gives and simply be obedient.

Brad, from the first story in this chapter, now working with Generous Giving, a national ministry, got wind of how Kyle was living and asked him to share his story of step-by-step obedience at their annual gathering of hundreds of people in Colorado Springs a few years ago. I flew out to encourage him the night before he spoke. We decided to room together—and I'm glad we did. It was great fun catching up. We talked and prayed until it was late.

Earlier in the day, I had asked him if he'd gotten the check my wife and I had sent for the coffee bikes, because we'd not received a receipt yet. "Yes, thanks," he said. "I appreciate it. The receipt went out this week."

As we turned out the light for the night, he was silent for a few moments and then said, "Clare, I lied to you. I haven't kept up with the receipting, and yours hasn't gone out yet. The second I told that lie I had a 10-Second Rule impression to confess it, but I didn't. I was afraid. But I just felt that same prompting again, so I needed to tell you. Please forgive me."

I broke down and quietly cried; I was so proud of

him. And I told him so. Men like that don't get built overnight.

The next morning, as he spoke of his trust in God and his faith journey, I suspect that every mother in the room was texting their unmarried daughters: *Get on the next flight to Colorado by noon!*

Jesus invites each of us to join this revolution of spontaneous obedience—the same one that Brad, Susan, Veti, and Kyle have been experiencing, saying in essence "Come follow me and see where I'll take you." But many of us, like the rich young ruler in the Gospels, are still sniffing around the trap, counting the cost—so wary that God will eventually ask us to do something radical that we never begin the journey, or instead choose some less costly religious activity, hoping it will be good enough.

In chapter 2, I pointed out that it's no wonder our kids are running for the church door when they leave high school, gagging on our hypocrisy because we give lip service to surrendering to the will of God, often with no real intention of doing so. If you're a parent or grandparent, your children are looking to you for a faith that works and that changes lives—that changes *you!*

Beware of sensible faith. A faith that does not compel you to occasionally risk personal loss or appearing foolish to your friends isn't Christian faith at all. I read this quote once, but for the life of me I can't remember where: *It's often the rich, the educated, and the religious who miss the call to follow Jesus, because it's an offense to their sensibilities.*

The Preparation

The School of Jesus

You all have a single Teacher, and you are all classmates.
Don't set people up as experts over your life, letting
them tell you what to do. Save that authority for God;
let him tell you what to do.

—MATTHEW 23:8–10, MSG

For years, one of my favorite TV programs was an intelligent and well-written drama, *The West Wing*, the story of the inner workings of the executive branch of government. The term *West Wing* refers to the section of the White House that contains the offices where the president's staff works. But the program was less about the daily functions of that staff than about how the personalities of the fictional staff in the program worked together (or failed to work) to make the presidency function.

On the show, Sam Seaborn was President Bartlet's speechwriter. When the president needed to deliver a speech—whether it was the State of the Union or an address to the Future Farmers of America—he turned to Sam. Rarely did he have to give Sam much direction. Sam had written or listened to almost every speech the president had delivered, and he had read almost everything President Bartlet had written. Sam sat around the edge of the president's conversations and meetings with cabinet members, congressmen, special-interest groups, and other staff, immersing himself in how the president spoke, how he handled himself—and how he handled others.

Sam knew the mind and heart of the president so well that he needed virtually no instructions to write his speeches. Sam could almost finish the president's sentences. He knew what the president believed and how he wanted his policies put into action. Sam could write with that level of confidence only because he had devoted himself to being a student of the president.

In one scene, the president is delivering an amazing speech—one that Sam had written. The audience, captivated, breaks into spontaneous applause. The president smiles broadly, then turns to Sam and gives him a wink, as if he were saying: *Well done, good and faithful servant.*

Apprenticing Yourself to Jesus

If you worked directly for the president of the United States—not in a fictional sense, but in real life occupying a desk in the West Wing of the White House—you'd never hear words like *balance* and *volunteer* with respect to your commitment to the president. You would be expected to do a whole lot more than simply attend weekly briefings to find out what the president was thinking, or listen to a few radio programs describing the president's agenda. You would be working for the most powerful person in the world, the person on whom the welfare of millions directly depends, and understanding what the president believes and wants, then carrying it out, would have to become *the* priority of your life.

Learning to pattern our lives after Jesus with ever greater confidence and courage will require nothing less. And when we seek to follow the 10-Second Rule, that's just what we're doing—patterning our lives after Jesus.

Even so, we don't have to look far to find Christians—lots of them, possibly including you and me occasionally—who seem to get by, or try to anyway, with Sunday briefings and minimal service—*good enough*. *Good enough* is kryptonite for every would-be follower of Jesus. It's the very source, the headwaters of lukewarm faith!

Good enough is what differentiates the religious from the sold out and surrendered, and is no more acceptable in following Jesus than it would be among the White House staff. The goal of our lives should be nothing less than becoming so familiar with the "mind of Christ" that we could write Jesus' speeches.

I invite you to apprentice yourself to Jesus, to become a student in the School of Jesus. Jesus himself, of course, will be your primary instructor. Let's discuss how that will work.

Observing Jesus

A few years ago I spent a few weeks in Israel learning what it actually meant to study under a rabbi. Many rabbis in Jesus' day had disciples. In fact, that's how many of them made their living—as teachers. But their teaching involved far more than information transfer.

Rabbis typically walked out front with their disciples, their *followers,* trailing close behind. As the rabbi walked, he would not only teach, but also stop and talk to people, buy things in the bazaar—conducting his normal, everyday activities. His disciples were expected to closely watch everything the rabbi did, because their goal was to become just like their rabbi. In fact, the success of a rabbi was often measured as much by the *character* of his disciples as it was the extent of their biblical knowledge.

Jesus is our rabbi. *To follow Jesus is to make the supreme purpose of our lives to become just like him.*

How do you follow your rabbi, to learn to live like him? Start by reading the Gospels. And when you do, take your time; read carefully; observe him. Mentally imagine yourself watching him, up close and personal, as he moves through the stories of the Gospels. When he speaks, assume that he's speaking to you, rather than the crowd. Ask yourself, *How would what he's telling me apply to my life today?*

For example, when you read in the Bible the words of Jesus such as "Love your enemies," stop and think of what that really means. That's harder than it sounds. We've read those words so many times before that our natural inclination is simply to agree: "Yes, I think we *should* love our enemies." But personalize it: How does Jesus want you to love *your* enemies?

Resist the easy response. This time, force yourself to ask and answer the tough questions. I'd suggest writing them down.

> Who are my enemies? Who really doesn't like me? Whom don't I like? Why?
>
> Who in the past has purposely made life difficult for me?
>
> How have I handled that hurt? Do I fantasize about what I'd like to do to that person?
>
> Have I gossiped about how I was treated? What should I do about that?
>
> Does Jesus really mean that I should *love* them? Isn't it enough to just forgive them, and not hold grudges?

Is *loving* more than that?

When was the last time I failed to love my enemy?

What could I have done differently?

In the same way, when you read Jesus' story of the persistent widow in Luke 18 regarding prayer, don't *just* read the story. Ask yourself questions like:

Why is Jesus telling *me* that story?

Is that how I pray?

Have I sometimes given up praying for something or someone just because I ran out of patience?

Is this story about prayer? Or is it more about faith?

Or is prayer an expression of faith?

Can I really wear God down by persistent prayer?

My point is that, especially since we've read them so often, it's easy to read these stories and forget to *savor* them, to *meditate* on them. One of the reasons God gave us Scripture is so that we can understand his heart, his will for the world. But so often we read the Bible as if it were just another interesting article, or some duty we have as Christians, one more thing to cross off our list. Meditating deeply on Scripture and then personalizing it is the best way I know to truly follow Jesus.

> *Take my yoke upon you and learn from me. (Matthew 11:29)*

And remember when reading the Bible, you're in no rush. Think of the School of Jesus as continuing education—it lasts a lifetime. So take a few days, even a week, to do some research on specific topics, then pray and seek counsel from those you trust. You'll want all the help you can get.

Now let me introduce you to the rest of the teaching staff.

The Holy Spirit

Jesus said that one of the Holy Spirit's ministries to us would be to *"teach you all things and . . . remind you of everything I have said to you"* (John 14:26). Also, *"He will convict the world of guilt in regard to sin and righteousness . . . and he will guide you into all truth"*—and *"he will glorify me because it is from me that he will receive what he will make known to you"* (John 16:8, 13, 14, NIV 1984).

The *"remind you"* ministry of the Holy Spirit is the one I find most fascinating. Like a spiritual Google search, the Holy Spirit brings to mind the things we've read in Scripture and actually helps interpret them for our use today. I urge you to take the time to read John 14, 15, and 16 to get a feel for the amazing ministry of the Holy Spirit!

When you think of the Holy Spirit, think of a wise attorney or trusted chief of staff who provides counsel you can trust. The Holy Spirit is your teacher! Before you do anything else each day, ask him to teach you, guide you, and increase your understanding in all matters of faith and life.

In 1 Corinthians 2:11, 12 and 16, Paul said, *"For who knows a person's thoughts except their own spirit within them? In the same way no one knows the thoughts of God except the Spirit of God. What we have received is not the spirit of the world, but the Spirit who is from God, so that we may understand what God has freely given us. . . . For who has known the mind of the Lord so as to instruct him? But we have the mind of Christ."*

As time goes by in this experiment in learning to discern God's voice, your confidence both in him and in yourself will grow as you practice listening and obeying. The Holy Spirit is Jesus' gift to you, so receive him with gratitude!

The Bible—for Life

When I was in college, I took biology as an elective. I read the textbooks and took notes during the lectures, but I had no plans to be a biologist. I saw no practical use for the information I was learning, so it went in one ear and out the other.

However, the premed students in the very same class had a whole different perspective. They studied the course material as if their future careers depended on it—because it did! The material taught in that biology class would be part of their life's work forever, and *that* made all the difference in the world.

And that—or even more so—is how we should read the Bible: as if it will be a part of our lives forever, guiding us, enlightening us, helping us in our studies in the School of Jesus. It is our only reliable source of spiritual and moral truth.

All Scripture is God-breathed and is useful for teaching, rebuking, correcting and training in righteousness, so that the man of God may be thoroughly equipped for every good work. (2 Timothy 3:16–17)

In the next chapter I'll urge you to consider reading the book of Luke over a thirty-day period, even as you begin living by the Rule. Once you've completed Luke, start in on the rest of the Gospels: Matthew, Mark, and John. Take all the time you need to study these wonderful teachings of Jesus more deeply. Personally, I try to read all four Gospels every year.

To help you get all you can out of your reading of the Gospels, here are some wonderful studies you may want to use as well:

> *Luke: Glory to God in the Highest!*, Woodrow Kroll (Crossway, 2009).
>
> *Luke: Lessons from Jesus*, Bill Hybels (Zondervan, 2008).
>
> *His Name Is Jesus: Life and Power in the Master's Ministry: A Study of Matthew, Mark and Luke*, Jack Hayford (Thomas Nelson, 1995).

And when you've completed your first read-for-your-life, in-depth study of the Gospels, turn your attention to the rest of the Scriptures. To really follow Jesus, you'll need to know the whole counsel of God—to know everything that God has tried to communicate to us in the Bible. Your goal is nothing less than building a biblical worldview for yourself, a practical, working theology that informs every moral or spiritual decision you'll ever make. The words the Lord put on the heart of Solomon thousands of years ago ring true even today: *"Store up my commands within you, turning your ear to wisdom and applying your heart to understanding . . . then you will . . . find the knowledge of God"* (Proverbs 2:1–5).

When Moses had delivered the words of the Lord to the Israelites, he said, *"Take to heart all the words I have solemnly declared to you this day, so that you may command your children to obey carefully all the words of this law. They are not just idle words for you—they are your life"* (Deuteronomy 32:46–47).

If you've not yet established a regular, daily time of prayer and Bible study, please make it a priority. I've never met a serious follower of Jesus who didn't, and I doubt you'll be the exception.

The Christian Community

This may sound almost heretical, but sometimes Bible study isn't enough.

The truth is, if I really just don't want to obey, I can always find something in Scripture somewhere to support my position. After all, *"The heart is deceitful above all things"* (Jeremiah 17:9). Remember, even Satan can quote Scripture! At times like that, when I suspect I'm just trying to justify myself, I often seek the counsel of others.

When you're uncertain about how Jesus' teachings apply to your life, ask someone you consider more spiritually mature for advice. God has given us the gift of community. We have a family of spiritual brothers and sisters, including our pastors, many of whom have far more experience and wisdom than we have. They'd be honored to help.

Why not use this incredible wealth of experience around you to help you mature in your obedience?

Spiritual Mentors

If you wanted to improve at playing the guitar, learning a foreign language, or any other skill, you'd probably find someone with experience and skill in that area who's willing to meet with you regularly. That mentor would demonstrate the skill you're trying to learn, teach you the theory behind it, answer your questions, and critique you as you try your hand at it. Why wouldn't you do the same for your Christian life?

Consider establishing a relationship with an older, more experienced teacher and friend in the Christian community, someone who would serve as your spiritual mentor. If that's your desire, you can get more information by going to our website and downloading a copy of *Spiritual Mentoring: A Guide for Finding and Being a Christian Mentor.*

Don't Wait!

As you've read this chapter, possibly realizing how much you have yet to learn, you may be tempted to hold off on obeying the 10-Second Rule until you've thoroughly studied and internalized everything. Please don't! As I said earlier, the School of Jesus is a lifetime commitment. You'll be studying how to think and act like Jesus until the day you die. Don't let your lack of full understanding keep you from obedience to what you're reasonably certain Jesus wants you to do today! For years my friends have heard me say, "I'm confident that if push comes to shove, Jesus would prefer that I was half as smart and twice as obedient!" So, go with what you know!

The only way we can truly authenticate ourselves as seekers and followers of Jesus is to measure ourselves by the life and teachings of Jesus. Not by our leaders or our doctrinal statement—just Jesus!

—FLOYD McCLUNG

---

*Floyd McClung, *Follow* (Colorado Springs, CO: David C. Cook, 2010), p. 13.

CHAPTER TEN

Doing the Rule: 10₄30

Just do it!

    —NIKE

I was first introduced to the Rule more than a decade ago. Bill Job, an amazing American pastor/businessman living in China, was meeting with a group of us about his work and almost offhandedly mentioned the Rule. We were so taken by his idea and his stories of how it had changed lives in unexpected ways that we agreed together to try to live by the Rule. Given that we were all a bunch of type-A guys, we figured that we would need all the help we could get as we tried to become more spontaneously obedient. So we prayed for God's wisdom, leading, and blessing before we began.

Each week, we gathered to tell stories of how God had spoken to us, impressing us to be more bold. Some weeks were incredibly inspirational and encouraging. At one of our better meetings, one member of our group reported that he'd seen another member with gas can in hand, helping a woman stranded by the side of the road. That inspired all of us to greater sensitivity to God's direction.

Other weeks, some of us would confess that we hadn't felt *any* impressions from God, or at least not as often as other weeks, or that we had chickened out, timid and unsure. On those occasions, we would commiserate a bit and then talk about what we might do differently, and better, next time.

It was exhilarating! It made our faith fresh, and the previously mushy concept of what it really meant to follow Jesus far more tangible. In many ways, it jump-started our spiritual lives. We felt the excitement of being new converts. And we were—converts to simple obedience.

Doing the Rule: 10₄30

Now it's your turn. I want you to prayerfully consider doing something similar to what our group did years ago. I want you to consider committing to *Doing the Rule: 10₄30*. That means living by the 10-Second Rule for (4) the next thirty (30) days—10₄30. You can do it individually, if that's what works best for you, or you can do what our group did in those early days—band together with others for mutual encouragement and accountability.

Yes, I know, it sounds like a serious commitment, and it is; you never know where it might lead at any particular moment. But regardless, can you think of a single good reason Jesus wouldn't want you to start obeying his leading today?

10₄30 is more than a commitment; it's also a plan. What does this plan include?

1. Pray for God's help.

I'd suggest that you commit the next thirty days to God by praying a prayer similar to this one:

Jesus, for at least the next thirty days I want desperately to live by the 10-Second Rule as faithfully as I can. I want to honor you and bless others by obeying you spontaneously and generously. Holy Spirit, I ask you to empower me with wisdom, opportunity, and courage to live out my faith with boldness and grace. I need you to help me do this. Please forgive me when I don't. Amen.

Just a word about this prayer. Humanly speaking, you already know that you can't obey the 10-Second Rule perfectly. You know that, and so does Jesus. This prayer is asking God's help to make you more faithful than you've ever been in your life. It's a promise of serious intention, not perfection.

2. Read the Gospel of Luke in thirty days.

If your goal is to listen to and obey Jesus, then the best place to start is by reading for yourself exactly what he did, what he said, and what others said about him. There are twenty-four chapters in Luke and you have a month to read them, so if you miss a few days over the next thirty, you can relax. This isn't a hard or detailed study. Just read to get a fresh perspective and greater appreciation of Jesus' character, of his love for the Father and for you, and of how he cared for hurting, lost, or marginalized people.

3. Courageously obey God.

A good definition of Christian faith is this: courageous obedience to the teachings of the Bible. And embedded in every act of courage is risk—doubt and fear are part of the package. Living by faith happens any time our obedience overrides our fears. Just commit yourself to doing the next thing you're reasonably certain Jesus wants you to do, as directed by him. Don't argue with it, don't overthink it—just do it!

4. Pray daily.

Pray for the routine events in your life: the people in your household you'll interact with in the next few minutes—people on the train or carpool, the people you work with, or the person whose locker is next to yours.

Pray for courage to be bold when God speaks.

If you have prayer partners, pray for them also.

Pray for the Holy Spirit to empower you to listen more attentively to his promptings.

Be attentive in case God speaks to you even during your prayers.

Asking the Holy Spirit for Guidance Daily

A friend of mine put me onto this idea as she began listening to God more intently for direction: Before she leaves home each day, she prays through her schedule. She visualizes herself leaving her apartment, entering her workplace, going to lunch, all the appointments of the day—everything she can think of until she goes to bed that night.

Imagine the people you expect to meet today. Do you have a meeting that might become difficult, maybe with an ex, or your boss, or a controlling parent, or a demanding customer? In the past, these emotional meetings may have triggered some very un-Christlike thoughts. But today, before you even leave the house, think through how Jesus would respond in these situations. Make any pre-decisions necessary to ensure that your actions and words will be more Christlike today. Pray that he'll soften your heart and prepare you to be Jesus in their presence.

Ask the Holy Spirit to give you "spiritual radar" for people on the fringe of your life. Envision, as you pray, the parent who stands alone at soccer practice, the people who eat by themselves at work or school, the barista at the coffee shop, the custodian at your children's school—people who may need a compliment or an encouraging word from God through you.

The Holy Spirit will guide you to opportunities—*and* he'll give you the words to say. As Jesus told his disciples, *"Do not worry about what to say or how to say it. At that time you will be given what to say, for it will not be you speaking, but the Spirit of your Father speaking through you"* (Matthew 10:19–20).

Be Bold!

Don't keep your 10₄30 commitment a secret. Let friends on Facebook know what you're doing, and why. Be vulnerable and honest. Tell them you're not doing this because you're a super Christian. In fact, it's because you're *not* that you're doing it. If they wonder what the Rule is, post a link to our website, where they can read a several-page description of the Rule for themselves.

Just think—your willingness to be spontaneously obedient may just be the catalyst for more intentional kindness, generosity, and holiness in your friends' lives.

The Blessing of Having a Prayer Partner

Humans were not meant to go it alone in this world, especially those who love God. Adam had Eve, and Moses, Joshua. David had Jonathan. Paul and Timothy were a team. Jesus even sent out his disciples in pairs, because *"Though one may be overpowered, two can defend themselves"* (Ecclesiastes 4:12). The reason sports teams have a home-court advantage is the powerful flow of energy and confidence that comes from thousands of fans screaming their encouragement.

As you can tell from my group's experience in the story that began this chapter, having a prayer partner will be a blessing for both of you. Why not begin praying soon for this Christian friend, or a group who might either do the Rule with you, or pray you through it?

Prayer partners might be best friends, siblings, spouses, or someone in a Bible study with you. They don't have to be spiritual giants. In fact, doing the Rule may just be how God shapes them into one.

If you do find a prayer partner, before you begin 10₄30, meet with your partner to talk it through. Be honest and vulnerable about questions and concerns you have, and encourage your partner to do the same. It would be helpful if both of you have read this book.

Once you've made your decision to go ahead, pray together and make plans to meet or contact each other weekly, if possible. Between these face-to-face meetings, plan on texting and using Facebook, email, or Twitter to share stories of what happened when you obeyed, and when you didn't. Promise that you'll be honest about your failures and that you'll contact each other when you're uncertain what to do. Pray for courage for one another.

Your First Pre-decision

We've talked throughout this book about the value of making pre-decisions about how to obey God in a variety of situations. If you've decided to live by the Rule for thirty days, this is where the rubber meets the road. Get at least one pre-decision in order now.

When you begin doing the Rule, there's a good chance that when you help someone, you'll be asked this question: "Why are you doing this for me?" Right now is the time to make some pre-decisions about how you're going to respond to this question. Here's an idea:

A. "I'm trying to live by the 10-Second Rule."

Q. "What's the 10-Second Rule?"

A. "Just do the next thing you're reasonably certain Jesus wants you to do."

Q. "And how do you know what Jesus wants you to do?"

A. "He tells us in the Bible, for one thing. But here's my problem: I've noticed that at times during the course of my day I will occasionally feel an impression to do something I'm reasonably certain Jesus wants me to do—or stop doing—like I just had with you. And I've found if I think about it too long, I usually talk myself out of it. So, by respond-

ing quickly, hence the '10 seconds,' I hope
to get better at obedience. The 10-Second
Rule is essentially a method to help me be
more like Jesus, and I still have a long way
to go."

From there, you can never be sure where the conversation will lead—but the Holy Spirit does, and he'll prepare you for whatever comes next. You can always direct
people to our website. There they'll find a helpful reading for non-Christians titled *God's Story*. It's a summary
of the entire Bible in less than a half-dozen pages with a
clear explanation of how interested people can become
followers of Jesus. There are also helpful resources and
links for Christians. Consider adding that interested person to your prayer list and pray for the Holy Spirit to
open their heart and mind to the love of God.

Making God Look Good

Here's how a friend of mine handles the inevitable
thank-you. Whenever a stranger thanks her for doing
something kind, she's careful to say, "Please don't thank

me—I sensed God wanted me to help and I'm simply trying to be obedient. So please just thank him."

"People who know me well don't need to hear that statement," she told me. "They know I love God. But I want every stranger to whom I'm kind or helpful to walk away thinking they've just been blessed by God himself."

What a great idea! And yet, in the first few years that I followed the Rule, I missed hundreds of opportunities to give God the glory—to make him look good. Instead, *I* took the bow. Now I, too, try to say something similar whenever I have the opportunity—to get myself out of the limelight.

Not to us, O LORD, not to us but to your name be the glory, because of your love and faithfulness. (Psalm 115:1)

$10_4 30$ for Churches

Can you imagine what could happen if your whole church—adults, high school and college students, even children—together decided to do the Rule?

In Charles Sheldon's book *In His Steps,* it was the senior pastor himself who was convicted to live for the next year by the answers to one question: "What would Jesus do?" That book, written more than a century ago, was the inspiration for the whole WWJD movement. That courageous pastor then challenged his entire church to do the same, and it transformed his church and the whole community. If you've not read this wonderful book, you'll want to.

Encouraging the leaders of your church to consider doing the Rule 10₄30 could be one of the greatest contributions you'll ever make to help revitalize the spiritual lives of your fellow members and fan into flames a movement of simple obedience.

A program to do that requires more than your suggestion to the church leaders, of course—it requires a plan, and it requires that you act on that plan. You'll find complete instructions for *Doing the Rule for Churches* on our website. You'll be surprised how simple it is and how profound its impact will be!

10$_4$30 for Families

Remember the story in chapter 8 about Brad and his family, how they worked together, even the children, to be an encouragement and blessing to people they came in contact with during the day? What a life-shaping experience that would be for a child, to grow up in such a family. What a powerful way to teach your children early just what following Jesus actually means.

So why not *your* family? Are you being impressed by God, even now, to do the Rule as a family? If so, on our website you'll find some wonderful ideas for including your children and spouse—just click on *Doing the Rule for Families.*

And if, once you and your family have tried it, you have stories of how your family obeyed Jesus and what happened when you did, we invite you to post them on our website.

Tools for Doing the Rule

On our website, you can download a large, 10-Second Rule image as wallpaper for your computer or phone. Not only will it serve as a good reminder for you, but when others see it, it will trigger conversations you might never otherwise have had. And while you're on our website, be sure to interact with others who are also trying the Rule by sharing your stories or responding to theirs.

At the back of this book, you'll find a study guide with questions and comments. You can use them on your own, with your prayer partner or for a group study. By using them, you will be reminded of the significant principles and practices behind the Rule that will help you live it out daily.

Keeping the Goal in Sight

I've been trying to live by the Rule as a lifestyle for about a dozen years now. The better I get at it, the more I realize how far I still have to go. I'm a fellow struggler in this journey of obedience, just passing on to you what I and others have learned—mostly through our mistakes! I don't yet have it nailed—I'm just confident that it's how Jesus wants me to live, and so I keep pressing on toward the mark.

You may be asking yourself just how often I obey

the Rule myself. I don't know . . . 40, 50 percent. Maybe. On a good day.

This is where grace shines. Nothing about our relationship with God is based on a percentage, or we'd give up altogether.

Every major-league baseball player knows that it's impossible to bat a thousand. A .325 batting average is unbelievable; most teams go through whole seasons without anyone on their team averaging that high.

What keeps a man in the game when he knows that two-thirds of the time he's going to fail? It's waking up each morning and believing that he can do better today than he did last year—and even yesterday—and then working hard toward that goal. If he ever stops believing in that possibility, and stops training hard to make that happen, he's done in the majors. Next year he'll be sent to the minor leagues. The year after that, he'll be selling used cars in Omaha.

Perfection in obeying Jesus is impossible. But with the Spirit of the living God in us, we can choose, every day, to do better than we did yesterday—better than we did last year. That much, we *can* do.

The day I settle for good enough, I'm halfway to Omaha.

> *But one thing I do: Forgetting what is behind*
> *and straining toward what is ahead, I press*
> *on toward the goal to win the prize for which*
> *God has called me heavenward in Christ Jesus.*
>
> —PHILIPPIANS 3:13B, 14, NIV 1984

CHAPTER ELEVEN

Why Bother?

The Bible is very easy to understand. But we Christians are a bunch of scheming swindlers. We pretend to be unable to understand it because we know very well that the minute we understand, we are obliged to act accordingly.

—SØREN KIERKEGAARD

You're almost done with this book. But it's time to honestly ask yourself why this revolution, this life-changing gospel begun by God himself, often feels more like a pilot light than a bonfire.

As you've been reading, there may have been a question forming in the back of your mind, one you'd be too embarrassed to discuss, even with your closest friend. It's one I've asked myself. And here it is: you're a good person and things are actually going pretty well. You gave your life to Christ at Camp Winnamonka when you were a kid, you attend church regularly and believe you're going to heaven, your life's not falling apart . . . besides just racking up more reward points, *why bother being more Christlike?*

Up to this point I've intentionally not said much about the benefits of obedience to us individually, for a reason. Yes, the Bible clearly teaches that God blesses, even rewards faithfulness. But I think we ought to trust him enough to let him decide just how and when he does that, and whether it's in this life or the next. That's what lovers do—they trust each other.

I'm wary of Christians who approach obedience with an attitude of "quid pro quo," expecting a specific blessing from God just because they've done something good for him or for another person. I wouldn't recommend picking up any Porsche brochures just because you wrote a generous check to your favorite ministry or even quit your day job to serve him full-time. That feels more like a transaction than obedience purely for love's sake and an unworthy motivation to "bother" following Jesus.

Words Wear Out

Some words wear out. It's not that they're wrong, simply that they've outlived their original meaning. I think the word *Christian* could be just such a word. It's a word that's nearly two thousand years old. In Antioch in the decades after Christ's crucifixion and resurrection, it was first applied to those who believed in Jesus and followed his teachings. And in the first few centuries of the church, when obedience was still costly, all Christians were also committed followers of Jesus—the terms were interchangeable. Today, all followers of Jesus are still Christians. But it's clear that the reverse is not true: Not all who call themselves Christians, even those sitting in church every Sunday, are truly his followers.

But exactly how do you define a follower of Jesus?

The answer to that question ought to be self-evident: Followers of Jesus have made it the priority of their lives to love God and be like Jesus.

How much of the time?

The underlying, unspoken question is this: "Just how good do I have to be to make God happy?" But my guess is that if we absolutely knew where that line was, we'd be content to be just barely over it.

Well, how about this definition: *"By their fruit you will recognize them"* (Matthew 7:20). Ah, that's how we can tell! The problem is, I've never yet met a totally fruitless Christian. Even the guy who does little more than show up at church, throw a ten in the offering plate, and volunteer in the children's department thinks he's fruitful.

The truth is, it's impossible to accurately measure our true devotion to God and our love for others. I don't have a faith-o-meter I can pull out every day and point at myself and others to keep score. Nevertheless, we do keep score, don't we? And it's the self-delusional nature of sin that causes us to believe we're better followers than most other Christians. Aside from the statistical impossibility of that being true, it's the wrong measure. The only true measure is Jesus.

There are two questions I've asked thousands of people in the past dozen years that blow through these smoke screens of comparison and excuses:

Based on how you live your life, what you're passionate about, how you care for others and spend your discretionary time and money, would your spouse, your children, or your closest friends characterize you as a Christian—or a serious follower of Jesus?

Then, forget for a moment what they think: Do you believe Jesus himself considers you one of his true followers?

He Looks So Lifelike!

Decades ago, when I was considering my break from cultural Christianity and truly following Jesus but not yet ready to take the plunge, I went to a pastor friend who knew me well. I gave him a litany of all the things I was doing: I taught Sunday school, served on mission boards, tithed regularly, believed every word of the Bible to be true. I was a nice guy! Ask anyone! (The Pharisees had nothing on me.) "So, what's wrong?" I asked. "What am I missing?"

"Clare," he said, "if you found a dead branch, stuck it in the ground, then wired apples to it and glued leaves on it, would you have an apple tree?" I almost laughed out loud before it began to sink in that he was describing me. I was the dead branch trying my best to look good to everyone, including God, without actually having surrendered my life to the lordship of Jesus. I wasn't trying to give God the glory and make him look good. The goal of my life was to make *me* look good!

At the time, my behavior and worldview were pretty much in sync with the Christian culture all around me. The problem was that *it*—the Christianity I was trying to mimic—didn't look anything like what Jesus required of his followers. It was a shallow counterfeit. And it was slowly dawning on me, sitting in church every Sunday, that although I was theologically certain, I was an obedience coward—no better than Peter. I could almost hear the cock crowing—this time for me!

I was an admirer of Jesus—I just didn't want to live like him or for him.

In fact, just the opposite. I treated God more like a spiritual rabbit's foot to be taken out and rubbed when life spun out of control. When the crisis passed, back into my pocket he went. In contemporary terms, God was an app on my iLife to be activated only when I needed him.

Just another form of grace abuse.

My life, like yours, belongs to God. We live to serve him, not the other way around. Do you believe that?

I started this chapter with the question: *Why bother?* Here's the answer: If you *really believe*—I mean truly believe you were created by God and saved by his Son and the Spirit of the living God is in you—why would you *not* want to spend the balance of your life fully devoted to him?

In fact, it dawned on me a while back that living by the Rule is simply the lowest common denominator for anyone who dares call him- or herself a follower of Jesus and claims to love him.

"Whoever has my commands and keeps them is the one who loves me. . . . Anyone who does not love me will not obey my teaching." (John 14:21a, 24a)

We don't like the idea of linking obedience to love, do we? We'd like to think of Jesus loving us unconditionally. But that's not the point of these verses. Jesus is telling us that obedience to *him* isn't a condition for his loving us, but it is the evidence of *our* love for him!

Breakfast with Jesus

Jesus posed similar questions to Peter after his resurrection, while fixing breakfast on the shore. Can't you just imagine Jesus down on one knee, tending the fire, probably looking like he did when he drew in the dirt with his finger before speaking in defense of the woman caught in adultery?

And as Peter approaches the fire, tired from fishing all night, he senses that something isn't right. Jesus isn't looking at him; he's thoughtfully staring into the fire and beyond. Then Jesus speaks slowly, as if choosing his words carefully, almost in a whisper so as not to shame Peter in front of the others.

"Peter, do you love me more than these?"

We're not exactly sure what Jesus meant by *these*.

Perhaps Jesus was asking whether Peter loved him more than he did the simple life of a fisherman, or the companionship of his friends, the good food frying in the pan, or the comfort of the familiar. Jesus was about to entrust his earthly ministry to eleven men. But this man, only days before, had denied he even knew Jesus—denied it three times! Now the Son of

Man needed to hear from him—to test him. Was Peter ready?

Three times Jesus asked a variation of this question.

Is it possible that Jesus didn't know the answer? Of course he did! Perhaps he wanted Peter, one last time, to count the cost, then shout his answer to Jesus out loud, leaving the sound of it ringing in the air and in his own ears.

Is Jesus still waiting for your answer? *Do you love me more than these?*

Is there something or someone else you love more than Jesus that's holding you back from fully following him? Your job? An addiction? The lifestyle you dream about? Hobbies in which you invest so much time and money? Friends you're afraid of losing? Your infatuation with your Facebook community? A boyfriend who's pulling you down? The comfortable routine of your Christian life?

Whatever grips your heart, whatever truly alters your behavior, that which you daydream about and talk about most with your friends—that thing is probably another god. I speak from experience. I'm embarrassed at how often my heart still stirs for gods I thought long dead.

Do you love me more than these?
Then come follow me.

Start Where You Are. Begin the Journey Today.

Even if your heart isn't yet fully committed, will you begin following Jesus again today?

Throughout history, Jesus has called ordinary Christians to revolutionary living, but few answer that call. You can choose today to be one of them, to take the road less traveled.

You've often heard the old Chinese proverb: "A journey of a thousand miles begins with the first step."

Don't think about how many steps you have ahead of you. The only important one is the next one. Just do the next thing . . .

Continue the Conversation

Please visit our website at www.the10secondrule.com—and while you're there, take the time to encourage others by posting your stories of living by the Rule on the 10-Second Rule page. You can also follow us and see what others are doing on Facebook at www.facebook.com/the10secondrule.

Our website also has a number of downloads and links to other websites and resources to introduce you to Jesus, or to help you truly live a revolutionary life!

And Without You . . .

At every stage in the writing and editing process I had family, friends, and gifted professionals encouraging me. When I finished my first draft, my wife, Susan, our children, Tim Stoner, and Joe Stowell were my early editing team.

A few of my wife's accountability partners, Meg Cusack, Betsy DeVos, and Julie Sikma, then went to work. They cured me of my "comma fetish" and made many other substantive suggestions and honest observations that occasionally made me wince. But once I let the air out of my ego, most of their ideas found a home in the manuscript.

Oh, and did I mention I don't use a computer to write? So every last word had to be typed from my hieroglyphics, handwritten on yellow legal paper and sticky notes by Ann Faber and Diane Luchies, my two patient administrative assistants.

I also have a special group of men around me—friends who have counseled me and have been some of the best friends a man can have. Without their support, you would not be reading this book. Ted Etheridge, Jerry Tubergen, Bill Payne, Dick DeVos, and the two other men in my accountability group, Brian Sikma and Bill Swets.

I'm also incredibly grateful for the talented people at the Somersault Group. This wonderful new company has a century of combined experience in the Christian publishing world, and I couldn't have received more spiritual or professional advice.

John Topliff, their general manager, is as godly as they get. Dave Lambert, my first editor, became my writing coach—a wonderfully gifted man who relentlessly drove me to write with greater and greater clarity. And I'm glad he did.

The first edition of this book was self-published, because I couldn't find a publisher who was willing to take a chance on a no-name author. Then my wonderful agents Robert and Andrew Wolgemuth introduced me to the amazing people at Howard Books—who immediately and truly believed in this book. Publisher Jonathan Merkh and editors Becky Nesbitt and Philis Boultinghouse became my team. However, it was Beth Adams, my final editor, who skillfully shaped the book you now hold in your hand.

And, above all, I thank God for inspiring and leading me and using the Christian community all around me to cheer me on.

Study Guide

I recommend you gather a few friends together for four weeks to read and discuss three chapters a week, including the introductory chapter. The discussion questions aren't about giving the correct answer—they're about discussing your honest answers, your fears, those things that keep us from simply obeying Jesus daily. The primary purpose for this study is to better understand the subtle reasons we've all used for not following Jesus. Once we understand that, we can begin building into our lives the habits of simple obedience that lead to authentic Christianity.

—*Clare De Graaf*

My Story—and Perhaps Yours As Well

1. What parts of the author's story can you most identify with?

2. If you, too, have experienced periods of "beige Christianity," what do you think contributed to them and what has led you out of them?

Chapter One: A Rule of Life

1. Discuss this quote: *"Using some internal moral-actuarial table, I would credit myself for church attendance, having personal devotions, giving, and generally being a good guy— with offsetting debits for sin. In my mind, and my arrogance, I assumed I had a positive balance compared to most other Christians I knew. I figured I had plenty of carry-forwards."*

Why is it most of us consider ourselves to be above-average Christians, and what effect does that have on your obedience?

2. What do you think of this observation by the author?

"I have a theory. I think we Christians who were once on fire for God often slowly and unconsciously drift toward religious activities, even good ones, because they're relatively convenient and culturally acceptable forms of obedience. It's a faith we can schedule into our busy lives—worship at 10:00 a.m., drop our offerings in the plate, Bible study on Tuesdays, volunteer on Wednesdays at 7:00 p.m. It's a spirituality that we can measure ourselves and others by—familiar and predictable, and it still leaves 95 percent of our waking hours for ourselves. Just the ticket for a user-friendly religion."

3. Can you recall the last time you waited for "a road to Damascus" experience from God before moving forward spiritually?

4. How do you think simply obeying the Rule might change your life? What scares you about doing that? If it does, why is it we find this kind of obedience so frightening?

Chapter Two: Dueling Voices

1. Can you recall the last time you sensed these "dueling voices" hard at work in you? What happened and how did you feel if you failed to respond well?

2. How would the first principle of the 10-Second Rule address your fears regarding obedience? *"When you're reasonably certain Jesus is asking you to do something, do it immediately!"*

3. Discuss this quote: *"Grace abuse is holding God to his promises while using them as an excuse to break our promises to him. Most of us wouldn't think of ourselves as actually doing that—but isn't that what we're really doing?"* Do you agree with the author that knowing you've been completely forgiven by Christ plays into your partial surrender? In what ways?

4. What do you think of the author's question *"But then you've just got to wonder what Jesus himself thinks when he hears us singing our hearts out in worship, 'I surrender all,' knowing full well that we have no real intention of surrendering all?"*

What other songs have you sung or worship habits have you gotten into that now feel gerbil-like and hypocritical?

5. Discuss the second principle of the Rule: *"The Rule gives you a place to begin again following Jesus, right now, and whenever you feel yourself drifting spiritually."* Has this actually helped you get back on track following Jesus again?

Chapter Three: Listening to the Voice of God

1. What's your reaction when someone says, "God told me . . . (whatever)"? How have you dealt with people who've made these proclamations of God's will? Has your skepticism of them made you wary of hearing from God yourself?

2. Discuss this quote: *"When I was a child, if one of my friends had said, 'Your mother told me she wants you to help the next person you meet who needs it,' I would have believed them. Given my mother's character, and how I've seen her treat people all her life, that sounds like something she'd do herself—*

and, therefore, like something she might ask of me. I wouldn't have had to personally hear her voice to confirm my friend's message. Her life was her voice. *So it is with Jesus' life."*

Is there someone you admire whom you know so well that you know intuitively how they would respond? Describe them and how their life encouraged you.

3. How could the third principle of the Rule be a breakthrough idea for you? *"The more you know about the teachings and character of Jesus Christ, the more confident you'll become following him."* Recall the last time your desire for certainty caused you to doubt and led to inaction.

4. Discuss the "standing orders" idea and the importance of obeying them consistently in order to build godly character. Have you found that even these standing orders can be ambiguous at times? If so, how has that played into your obedience or disobedience?

5. In what ways have you found the fourth principle of the Rule freeing? *The Rule doesn't require that you be absolutely certain an impression is from God before you obey.*

6. Do you think the author's warnings about not using the Rule for major decisions are valid, or could they be one more hindrance to obeying Jesus? Do you know someone who made a serious decision based on impulsively following "the leading of the Holy Spirit" and lived to regret it?

Chapter Four: Why Your Simple Obedience Matters

1. Discuss this quote: *"As a member of God's family, your mission in life is to be Jesus' stand-in. That means he expects you to behave like him—as if he lived in your house, raised your children, saw the same strangers and needy people you see, and hung out with your friends. More than that—it's intentionally living with your spiritual radar full on, eagerly anticipating his next assignment."* Describe what you think it means to live with your spiritual radar full on.

2. Discuss this quote: *"There's a reason Jesus asks us to do these 'divine chores' in the family of God. As spiritual children, simple obedience to his requests like the Rule gets things done* *in the household of faith, or the kingdom of God, that we can't possibly understand now or maybe ever."*

Talk about the chores you were asked to do when you were young that shaped you in ways beyond just getting those tasks done.

3. Discuss the fifth principle of the Rule. *"Christian character is shaped less by your big, dramatic decisions than by the cumulative impact of thousands of small acts of simple obedience."* Have you noticed that to be true in your life?

4. Discuss your ideas for training yourself to be godly prior to reading *The 10-Second Rule*. How did you attempt to do this? Was it "information gathering" (like the Bible studies), better sin management, or intentional character-building activities like serving others? Or all three? Which were the most effective?

5. Discuss this quote: *"In our day heaven and earth are on tiptoe waiting for the emerging of a Spirit-led, Spirit-empowered people. All of creation watches expectantly for the* *springing up of a disciplined, freely gathered, martyr people who know in this life the life and power of the kingdom of God. It has happened before. It can happen again"* (Richard Foster).*

Do you know anyone like that? What do you think Foster means when he uses the phrase "martyr people"?

Chapter Five: The Power of Small Beginnings

1. Can you identify with the author's discomfort with "risking himself" for God? When did that last happen to you and how did it feel?

2. What's the next thing you're reasonably certain Jesus wants you to do to serve the kingdom of God or grow personally as a Christian that you've been reluctant to do?

3. What "big things for God" have you dreamt about doing? Can you identify with the author's admission?

---

*Richard Foster, *Celebration of Discipline* (San Francisco: Harper & Row, 1978), p. 150.

Have you too dreamt about being admired for doing them? Are there some smaller things you probably need to do first to prepare yourself to follow Jesus in this area that you've been putting off?

Chapter Six: Pre-decisions

1. Why do you think you failed the last "pop quiz" that you were reasonably certain God sent your way? Do you think a pre-decision would have made any difference?

2. Prior to reading this book, had you ever thought about making pre-decisions? If so, discuss some you've made.

3. Do you have any written boundaries for your life? If so, please share them with the group. How have they been helpful?

4. Why is it that we rarely think of spending money on ourselves as "wasting it"?

5. Why is it so hard to deal with habitual sin, or "pet sins"?

Chapter Seven: Love the One You're With

1. Have you ever slotted people into "worthy and less worthy" categories, and why do we do that? Are there other ways you *sort* people?

2. Do you think it's all right to serve someone, even if your heart isn't in it? (After you've discussed this, read Matthew 21:28–32.) What does this passage teach us about that?

3. Do you think it's possible that God loves us, but at times doesn't "like us" because of our behavior? Were there times God didn't *like* the Israelites in the desert but still loved them as his own and cared for them? What application does that have for us? Is there someone you don't like whom God may want you to love?

4. Have you had to set some personal boundaries to make sure you're not just enabling a person you're really trying to help? Do you feel guilty when you say no, even for the right reasons? Why is that?

5. Discuss this quote: *"The risk-averse will rarely follow Jesus. Being taken advantage of occasionally is the occupational hazard of a servant."* What risks do you fear taking the most?

6. Do you think some people are "natural servants"? Do you think "that's not the way I'm wired" is a reason not to get involved?

Chapter Eight: From a Rule to a Lifestyle

1. Do you think it's true that we (you) have lived Christianity more as a religion to be believed than a revolution to be lived? How do revolutions start? Has yours begun? Do you want your children to be the "revolutionary" you are or do you hope for more? What can you do to inspire them to do that?

2. What person's story could you most identify with: Brad's intentional obedience, Susan and Veti from Albania, or Kyle's simple obedience? Why?

3. Did you have a parent or grandparent who lived like one of these people? If so, do you think they were intentional about it, or was it simply their lifestyle? Can you identify the virtuous habits they had that inspire you?

4. Would the people who know you best consider you a *grace dispenser*?

5. Kyle was reluctant to admit he lied. Why is it we find confession so difficult?

Chapter Nine: The School of Jesus

1. What message are you sending God by the time you invest in Bible study and prayer weekly, compared to the other ways you spend your discretionary time?

What might he conclude about what's really important to you?

2. Discuss the Bible study method taught in this chapter. Have you tried it? Does it work for you? Is there another method that works better for you?

3. Do you have a spiritual mentor? What might be the value of having a mentor, and how would you go about finding one?

4. Do you agree or disagree with this statement? *"If push comes to shove, Jesus would prefer that I was half as smart and twice as obedient!"* As important as Bible study is, talk about the danger of substituting information accumulation for true obedience.

Chapter Ten: Doing the Rule 10,30

1. Have you made a decision to do the Rule yet? If so, share how it's going. If not, what's still holding you back?

2. Do you have a prayer partner? Do you think it would be easier to follow the Rule if you had one? Why?

3. When someone asks you why you are doing something kind or generous for them, are you prepared for what will you say? (Why not practice your response to each other right now?)

4. How do you think praying through your schedule every day would affect your sensitivity to the Holy Spirit's leading?

5. Have you sensed God asking you to be the champion for *Doing the Rule* in *your* church?

Chapter Eleven: Why Bother?

1. What do *you* think is the difference between a Christian and a follower of Jesus?

2. In what ways have you tried to "wire apples and glue leaves" on your Christian life so you'd look good to those around you?

3. Honestly, if you lived your life as if it truly belonged to God, how would it look different than it does today?

4. Discuss the passage from John 14:23a, 24, regarding how God knows we love him.

5. Is there anything you love more than Jesus? Don't be quick with your answer; this is the most important question in the book. Imagine yourself standing by the fire. What would give Jesus pause about your claim to love him above all else?

6. What is the next thing you're reasonably certain Jesus wants you to do?